The **Wrigley** Family

A Legacy of Leadership in Santa Catalina Island

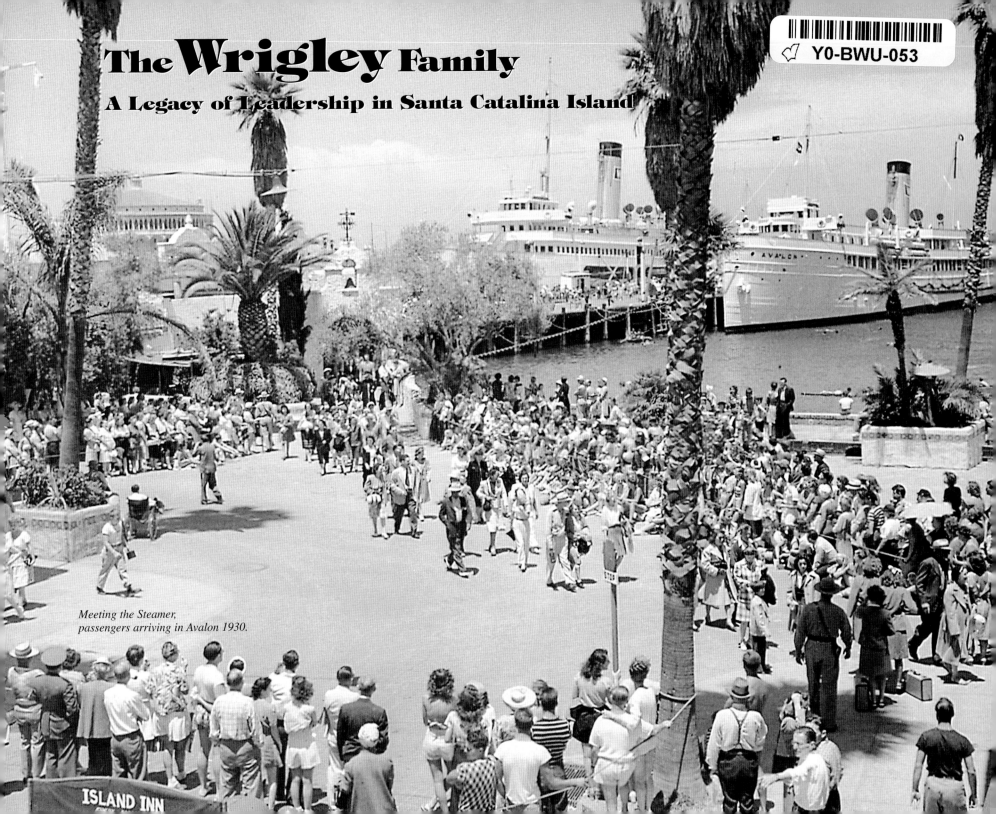

Meeting the Steamer, passengers arriving in Avalon 1930.

⁘ DEDICATION ⁘
BY WILLIAM SANFORD WHITE

This book is dedicated to the Wrigley family, past, present, and future, and their entrepreneurial spirit in the care and development of Santa Catalina Island. Their courage to stay the course in its protection and their continued commitment to its magic, its people and its history have made Catalina a Magic Isle.

Look around the Island today and you will see the human touch of the Wrigley family everywhere. From the landmark Casino that greets the one million visitors to Avalon each year, to the Wrigley Institute for Environmental Studies hidden away at Two Harbors, you will find the Wrigley hand at work – a testament to their all-encompassing generosity and devotion to Santa Catalina Island and the generations of people who continue to treasure this little piece of paradise.

Published and Distributed by
White Limited Editions and White Family Trust
Mailing Address: P.O. Box 126, Glendora, CA 91740
phone 626.335.8730   fax 626.963.9818
Business Address: 209 Descanso Avenue, Avalon, CA 90704
phone 310.510.1338

Also published by the author
"Santa Catalina Island – Its Magic, People and History"
"Santa Catalina Island Goes To War – World War II – 1941-1945"

Electronic Communications
Kim Lianne Stotts

Graphic Production
Robbie Bos, Mountain Creative Services, Big Bear Lake, California

Printing
Pace Lithographers, Inc., City of Industry, California

ISBN: 0-9659793-4-2
Copyright © 2005 by William Sanford White DBA White Limited Editions

Front & Back Covers
painted by master artist
John V. Partridge

William Wrigley Jr.
1861-1932

Philip Knight Wrigley
1894-1977

William Wrigley
1933-1999

FOREWORD

The Wrigley family and Catalina Island have had a close personal relationship for many years.

It all began in 1919. Enchanted by the idea of owning and developing a Pacific island so close to the family home in Pasadena, William Wrigley Jr. seized the opportunity to purchase Santa Catalina Island. Unique for that era, his vision of a vacation spot that would be available to all, regardless of economic or social status, laid the foundation for what Catalina was to become.

His son, my father, Philip Knight Wrigley, accepted stewardship of the island in 1932 and spent the next 45 years enhancing the transportation, residential, recreational, and ecological facilities of the island. In 1977, responsibility for the new Catalina passed to the next William Wrigley, my brother, Bill, who accepted the increasing complexity of administering the island's many aspects and forged enduring relationships with ecological research and conservation organizations.

Today, descendants of the Wrigley family are still very much involved in shaping Catalina Island's future. The basic principles held by my grandfather, William Wrigley Jr., in 1919, have been passed on through the generations, along with a genuine love for the island. Expanding on the material covered in Bill White's previous book, *Santa Catalina Island: Its Magic, People, and History*, this book focuses on the Wrigley family-particularly those who have led the island to its current position as an internationally recognized vacation resort, nature reserve, and ecological resource. Each of these men, in his own style, has left all of us a priceless legacy.

This Island, whose magic has touched so many, is also indebted to its native sons and daughters. Among these, William S. White has generously used his ability, knowledge, and time to chronicle Island history and people in his series of books about Santa Catalina Island. Thank you, Bill White. "Well Done!"

BY ADA BLANCHE WRIGLEY SCHREINER

Santa Catalina Island

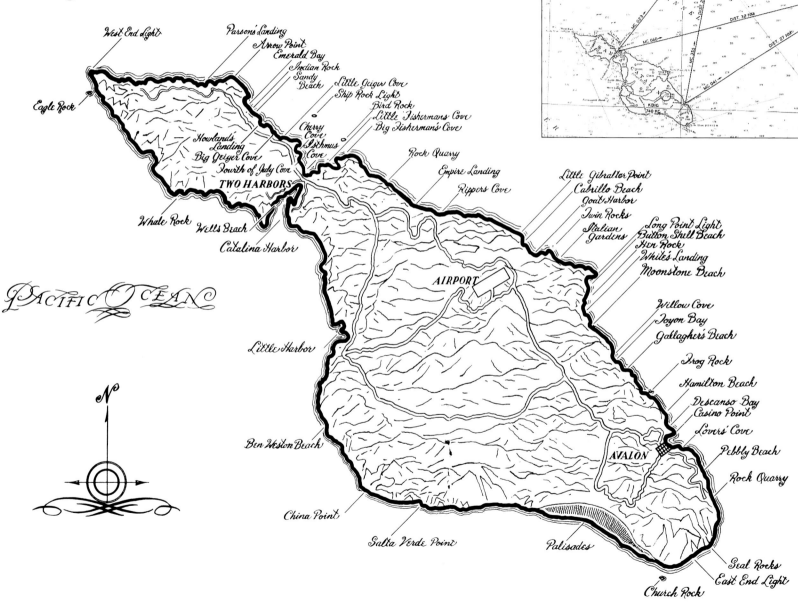

West End Light
Parson's Landing
Arrow Point
Emerald Bay
Indian Rock
Sandy Beach
Little Geiger Cove
Ship Rock Light
Bird Rock
Little Fisherman's Cove
Big Fisherman's Cove
Eagle Rock
Howland's Landing
Big Geiger Cove
Fourth of July Cove
Cherry Cove
Isthmus Cove
Rock Quarry
Empire Landing
Little Gibraltar Point
Cabrillo Beach
Goat Harbor
Rippers Cove
Twin Rocks
Italian Gardens
Long Point Light
Button Shell Beach
Hen Rock
White's Landing
Moonstone Beach
TWO HARBORS
Whale Rock
Wells Beach
Catalina Harbor
AIRPORT
Willow Cove
Toyon Bay
Gallagher's Beach
Frog Rock
Hamilton Beach
Descanso Bay
Casino Point
Lovers' Cove
Pebbly Beach
Rock Quarry
Little Harbor
PACIFIC OCEAN
N
Ben Weston Beach
AVALON
China Point
Salta Verde Point
Palisades
Seal Rocks
East End Light
Church Rock

Wrigley

The English surname Wrigley is of local origin, being one of those names derived from the name of the place where the original bearer once lived or owned land. In this case, it is derived from the placename Wrigley-Head, in Lancashire. This surname would therefore have simply identified the original bearer as a "local of Wrigley". Early instances of this surname include one William de Wriggley, who lived in Derbyshire in 1327 (Subsidy Rolls) and one Willelmus de Wryglegh, whose name was recorded in the Hundred Rolls for Yorkshire in 1379. More recent records reveal that a Thomas Wrigley (1808-80) was High Sheriff of Lancashire in 1872 and John Basil Wrigley (1882-1963) as High Sheriff of Cumberland in 1932. This surname has also been recorded as that of some notable English families (Kelly's Handbook to the Titled, Landed and Official Classes). In England, the surname Wrigley is most numerous in Lancashire, Cheshire and Westmoreland. Notable bearer of the name was American businessman William Wrigley, Jr. (1861-1932), the world's greatest producer of chewing gum. The surname has been documented in Ireland. Joseph Wrigley and family were Irish passengers bound for New York in 1848. (The Famine Immigrants)

BLAZON OF ARMS : Or, on a chevron sable three mullets of the field between two flaunches gules each charged with a stag's head erased of the field.

Translation : The mullet, or five-pointed star, denotes Honour and Achievement, while the stag is the symbol of Purity, Longevity and Fleetness.

CREST : A stag's head or semee of mullets sable holding in the mouth a trefoil slipped vert.

ORIGIN : England.

Verification of Authenticity affixed by signature of H.R.C. Consultant

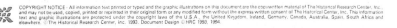

0806/0-29428

Warmest
Regards!!
White
Sanford

William

2009

☞ PREFACE ☜

THE LEGACY OF A FAMILY BUSINESS:
WILLIAM WRIGLEY JR., PHILIP WRIGLEY, AND BILL WRIGLEY

William Wrigley Jr. founded his company in 1891 at age twenty-nine. During its early years the firm grew slowly. In 1899, Mr. Wrigley overcame pressure to join a "trust" of six larger chewing gum makers who hoped to squeeze small independents out of business. He had a vision for the company, and did not want to give up control to an industry conglomerate. Between 1900 and 1910, the company's market share steadily increased, and by the close of that decade, Wrigley's Spearmint gum was America's favorite. In 1919, William Wrigley Jr. purchased control of the Santa Catalina Island Company and a seventy-six square mile mountainous island located approximately twenty-two miles west of Los Angeles in the Pacific Ocean.

In 1925, after thirty-four years at the helm, William Wrigley Jr., stepped down, and the presidency of the gum company passed to his son, Philip. The personalities of the two men were starkly different. William enjoyed the limelight and liked being at the center of the action. Philip was quiet and somewhat introspective. They were alike in that both kept the company on a steady course of success. Philip made real sacrifices for the good of the nation during World War II and, as owner of the Chicago Cubs, stuck to his belief that restricting baseball to daytime improved the quality of life for residents around Wrigley Field.

In 1961, at age 66 – just two years older than his own father had been at retirement – Philip Wrigley stepped down and his son Bill became president and CEO of the gum company. Bill Wrigley had never known his grandfather, having been born the year after his passing; but like both his grandfather and father, he maintained a steady hand at the tiller. Bill Wrigley, whose personal fortune exceeded $2.7 billion according to his 1999 obituary in the *Chicago Sun-Times*, was "quiet, shy…and unfailingly polite" – unlike the brash, ill-mannered billionaires we hear of today. He was in charge of the company's day-to-day operations for 38 years, longer than either of the earlier Wrigley chiefs. (William Jr., led the Wrigley Company for 34 years, Philip for 36.)

The Wm. Wrigley Jr. Company became one of America's most successful businesses very early in the 1900s and remained successful throughout the century. The company had just three leaders in the 108 years before Bill Wrigley's passing in 1999. Each of the three men had overcome different challenges: dominance by a conglomerate, two World Wars, the Great Depression, several recessions and, late in the century, the "corporate raider" phenomenon.

Among the characteristics that have endeared the Wrigley family to Catalina Island; to Chicago, the company's hometown; and to all of America has been what the *Sun-Times* called its "strong civic conscience," and the "care, caution and low-key efficiency" with which it has run its company. Now that legacy moves into the 21st Century under the stewardship of William Wrigley, Jr. for the WM. Wrigley Jr. Company, and Paxson H. Offield and Alison Wrigley Rusack for the Santa Catalina Island Company – the great-grandchildren of the founder.

The Wrigley Family
A Legacy of Leadership on Santa Catalina Island Since 1919

☞ TABLE OF CONTENTS ☜

William Wrigley Jr.
Born 1861 – Died 1932
The Beginning of the Legacy

ISLAND ACHIEVEMENTS – 1919 to 1932

Change of Ownership – Bannings to Wrigley

Wrigley Family Home Built on Mt. Ada

Cross-Channel Transportation, Terminal and Steamships
Opened Wilmington Mainland Passenger & Freight Terminal
Purchased SS Avalon Steamship
Launched SS Catalina Steamship

Hotels & Residential Housing Developed
Expansion of St. Catherine Hotel & Sugarloaf Casino
Hotel Atwater & Arcade Building
Island Villas & Bungalows replace Tent City
Sold Land and Homes to Private Citizens
SCI Employee & Tremont Street Housing

Tourism Development
Excursions – Motorcoaches, Glass Bottom Boat, etc.
Hollywood Movie Star Playground at Isthmus & Coves
Catalina Country Club Golf Course Expanded to 18-holes
Sport Fishing, Horseback Riding & Island Hunting

Business Development
Catalina Pottery & Tiles, Furniture Shop & Factory
Agricultural Products – Fruits, Vegetables, Poultry, Hogs
Ranching – Horses, Cattle, Goats & Sheep
Quarry Operations at Pebbly Beach –
    Silver Mining at Blackjack, Renton Mine, and Empire Landing

Entertainment
The Casino Ballroom, Big Bands & Movie Theater
Catalina Bird Park Aviary
Chicago Cubs – Spring Training at the Island
Chimes Tower, Clock & Music
Wrigley Ocean Marathon (Catalina to San Pedro)

Education & Public Utilities Improvement in Avalon
Avalon Public School Buildings & Education
Fresh Water Supply & Distribution System
Thompson Dam and Wrigley Reservoir
Public Utilities – Electric, Gas, Petroleum & Sanitation
Communications – Telegraph & Telephone

Celebrated Residents & Famous Visitors

Wrigley Managers & Administrators
Joseph & Son, Milton Patrick
David & Son, Malcolm Renton
Ernest & Son, John Windle

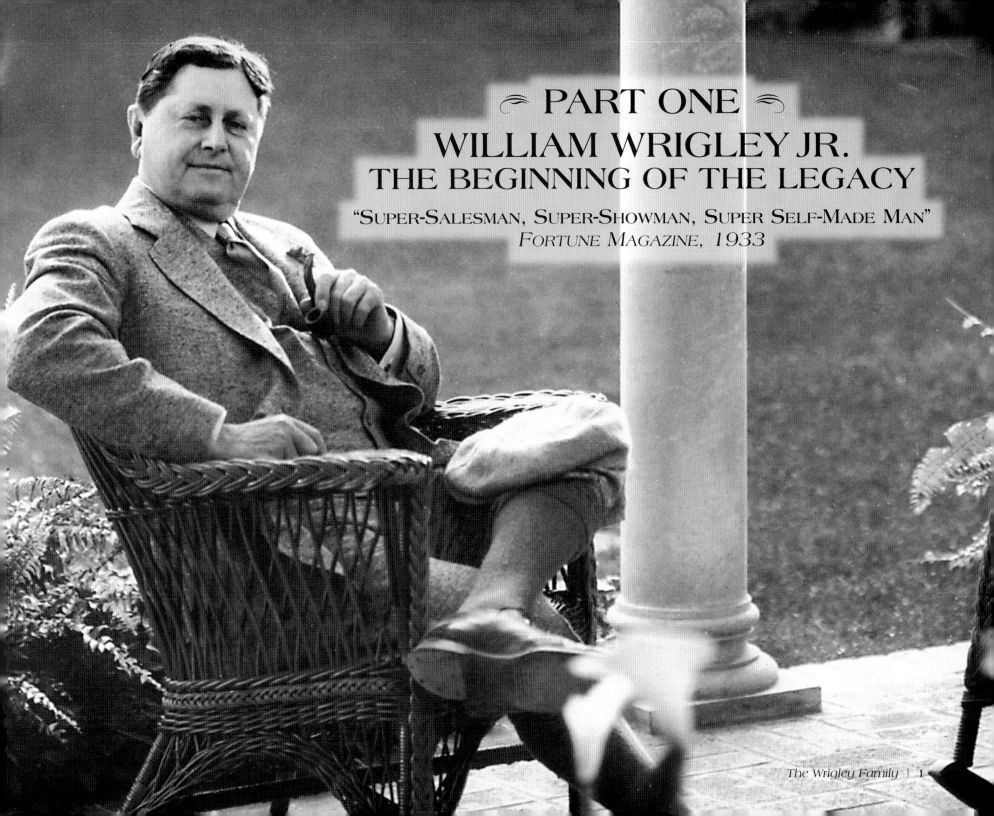

PART ONE
WILLIAM WRIGLEY JR.
THE BEGINNING OF THE LEGACY

"SUPER-SALESMAN, SUPER-SHOWMAN, SUPER SELF-MADE MAN"
FORTUNE MAGAZINE, 1933

⸙ BACKGROUND OF A LEGACY ⸙
WILLIAM WRIGLEY JR. FAMILY PRE-1919

William Wrigley Jr. at the age of 3.

William Wrigley, Sr., president of the Wrigley Manufacturing Company, and father of William Wrigley Jr.

The oldest of five children, William Wrigley Jr. was "born in the rebellion" five months after the start of the Civil War on September 30th, 1861, to William and Mary Wrigley of Philadelphia. His father enlisted in the Union army and served as an officer of the Pennsylvania Infantry until his honorable discharge.

When young William was eight or nine, his father began the Wrigley Manufacturing Company, selling Wrigley Scouring Soap. The post-Civil War era was a time of rapid growth in the United States, and the business was generally successful.

The summer he was eleven, William Wrigley Jr. and a friend took a train to New York City, where they worked at various jobs, hoping to create their own "rags-to-riches" story. The following year, Wrigley Jr. went to work in his father's soap factory, soon going on the road with a wagon and horse team as a salesman. He quickly became adept at salesmanship, and by the time he reached his 20s, he was ready to put some of his own merchandising ideas into practice.

Packages of chewing gum were offered as premiums when customers purchased Wrigley's soap.

William Wrigley Jr.,
principal owner and developer of Santa Catalina Island, 1919-1932.

Ada Foote Wrigley,
wife of William Wrigley Jr.

Mr. and Mrs. Wrigley Sr. seated, with their children in Philadelphia, 1891. Standing left to right: Charles, Anna, William Jr., Byron, and Edward.

William Wrigley Jr.

William met his future wife Ada Elizabeth Foote, and courted her for almost two years before marrying in September of 1885. William was twenty-three and Ada was eighteen. In 1891, William and Ada moved to the fast-growing city of Chicago to start a new business, the William Wrigley Jr. Company, with William's cousin William Scatchard, Jr. The main product was soap, and sales began along the same line as his father's had. The company grew slowly in its first decade, but eventually Mr. Wrigley's innovative ideas and persistence paid off. Wrigley was certain that promotional material, especially "gift" premiums to accompany deliveries would be effective in stimulating sales. These premiums generated substantial interest. Eventually, a fateful offer was tried: "Buy one can of baking powder – receive two packages of chewing gum, free!" It was soon clear from the response that the gum was every bit as popular as the baking powder. So began the Wrigley chewing gum business. By 1910, Wrigley's Spearmint gum was America's favorite.

Rare Wrigley's Gum advertising art.

Ada Elizabeth Wrigley and William Wrigley Jr.

In the 1910s, Mr. Wrigley began to fully express his business creativity. In 1915, he purchased a mansion in sunny Pasadena on South Orange Grove Boulevard, then known as Millionaires' Row. The home, designed by Lawrence Stimson, remained in the Wrigley family until the death of Mrs. Ada Wrigley in 1959, when it was donated to the City of Pasadena. It has long been the headquarters of the Tournament of Roses Association.

In January 1916, Wrigley and a group of other investors purchased the Chicago Cubs baseball team. After purchasing Catalina, he moved their spring training to Avalon. Around the same time he invested in a Pacific Coast League Team named the Los Angeles Angels.

While all of these capital outlays cut into his fortune, Wrigley was enjoying his wealth, and often directing it toward the welfare and pleasure of others. "The only real joy in business is the joy of creation. Making money in itself doesn't amount to a hill of beans," he said.

The Chicago Cubs at the spring training ballpark in Avalon around 1930.

The Wrigley Mansion in Pasadena, now the headquarters of the Pasadena Tournament of Roses and Rose Bowl football game each New Year's Day.

Rose Parade float entry for Catalina Island.

WM. WRIGLEY JR. COMPANY

WRIGLEY BUILDING
400 NORTH MICHIGAN AVE.

OFFICE OF
CHAIRMAN OF THE BOARD   CHICAGO   June 12th,
                                                        1 9 2 5.

Mr. Newton Sample,

Fallbrook, California.

Dear Mr. Sample:

            Your letter of
May 31st arrived in Chicago during
my absence abroad and I only came
in contact with same today.

            I enjoyed very
much reading the poem. I hope
some day to be exiled on Catalina
Island myself. At the present time
it takes so much money to keep up
with the development that I have
to stay somewhere else and earn it.

            Very truly yours,

THE LEGACY BEGINS
WILLIAM WRIGLEY JR. AND SANTA CATALINA ISLAND

When William Wrigley Jr. asked real estate broker David Blankenhorn his trademark question, "Well, what are you up to today?" he probably couldn't imagine that the answer would lead him to purchase an island. Blankenhorn was "trying to sell an island in the Pacific" for the Banning brothers, William, Hancock, and Joseph. After a little conversation and the viewing of some colored postcards of Catalina, Mr. Wrigley joined in a syndicate arrangement for the purchase, sight unseen.

Two weeks after the sale, Mr. and Mrs. Wrigley took the steamer to Avalon to see what they had purchased. A heavy fog drifted over the channel, obstructing their view, as they made their way 22 miles from the mainland. As they neared Catalina, the fog lifted, and Mr. Wrigley exclaimed, "My goodness. It's a mountain. I thought it was flat."

On their first visit, the Wrigleys stayed at the recently constructed St. Catherine Hotel in Descanso Canyon. Later, Wrigley vividly recalled the first morning they awoke on Catalina Island.

"My wife and I were both early risers and that morning Mrs. Wrigley was up first. She walked to the window and after a moment called excitedly, 'I should like to live here.' I joined her at the window. The sun was just coming up and I had never seen a more beautiful spot. Right then and there I determined the island would never pass out of my hands."

Ada Elizabeth, William Wrigley Jr. and Helen Atwater Wrigley at the Santa Fe Train Station in Pasadena. A gentleman named Blankenhorn met with William Wrigley, Jr. to share the availability of Santa Catalina Island for purchase.

Ernest Windle's "History of Santa Catalina Island, a guide to many of the little known 'high lights' of the 'magic isle'", *second edition.*

In 1919, William Wrigley Jr., along with two other investors, David Blankenhorn and Robert Hunter, purchased Santa Catalina from the Banning brothers. The exact events of the 1919 transfer of ownership are not completely clear. Two stories have been passed along through the decades. One says that the papers were reviewed and signed at Judge Joseph Banning's home at Catalina's Isthmus. Another states that the signing took place at David Blankenhorn's Los Angeles office. The lovely hacienda-style home Banning built in 1909 would certainly have been a more scenic location. (The house still stands high on a ridge overlooking the village of Two Harbors.) Confusion may have resulted if some documents were formalized at one location, while others were signed at another.

A booklet written by Ernest Windle and published by the *Catalina Islander* in 1940 offers a tantalizing clue. His description of William Wrigley Jr.'s purchase of Santa Catalina Island, is accompanied by a photo of Wrigley and Captain William Banning sitting together on the patio of the Banning home. Could this be the actual signing of the deeds?

WINDLE'S HISTORY OF SANTA CATALINA ISLAND (WITH MAP)

SECOND EDITION

By ERNEST WINDLE

A GUIDE TO MANY OF THE LITTLE KNOWN "HIGH LIGHTS" OF THE "MAGIC ISLE."

Published by THE CATALINA ISLANDER
Avalon, Santa Catalina Island, California
ALL RIGHTS RESERVED
COPYRIGHT 1940

... months were very

... lots the Santa Catalina Island Company leased 20-foot residential lots at a rental of $25 per year, and lessees built flimsy wooden structures or tents that could be taken down at the end of their vacations.

A cement sidewalk had been built along Crescent avenue and a 30-foot roadway was constructed from Avalon to the Hotel St. Catherine along the waterfront, around Sugar Loaf Point, where now stands the Casino.

Capt. A. B. Waddingham was appointed city engineer after the incorporation in 1913 and held that position until he volunteered his services in the World War. As engineer for the Banning Company, he surveyed the streets and made the various maps that later became part of the legal description of the town of Avalon.

Under the Banning regime, the population of the town during the month of August, the most popular month of the summer, frequently exceeded 5000; during the winter months the number would dwindle to about three or four hundred.

William Wrigley Jr. Buys Catalina

Early in January 1919, Captain David Blankenhorn, a real estate broker of Pasadena, interested Mr. William Wrigley Jr. in the possibilities of purchasing Santa Catalina and operating it as a pleasure resort. Concerning the incident, Capt. Blankenhorn said: "One morning I met Mr. and Mrs. Wrigley at the Santa Fe Station in Pasadena. It was when they were running a DeLuxe train in 1919. Mr. Wrigley saluted me, as usual, in that wonderful and enthusiastic way he had and said, 'Well, David, what are you doing?'

"My answer was that I was trying to sell an island in the Pacific called 'Catalina'.

"He said: 'I have never seen it but I would like to talk with you about it. Come up if you are not busy. I will be home in a few minutes.'

"I went around to a bookstore and got some colored post cards of Catalina, drove up to the Wrigley residence on Orange Grove Avenue. Mr. Wrigley said, 'How much money do you need to close the deal?'

"I had formed a syndicate for the purchase of the island; then I told him how much was needed.

"That noon I had the principal papers signed for the purchase of Santa Catalina all within three hours after the time he arrived in Pasadena.

18

William Wrigley Jr.   **Capt. William Banning**

"About two weeks later Mr. and Mrs. Wrigley made their first trip to the Island. We happened to be on the Hermosa, a small boat which has now been discarded. As the fog lifted, Mr. Wrigley said, 'My goodness, it is a mountain. I thought it was flat'.

"It has always been a consolation to know how much he loved the Island and how much he enjoyed its development; the City of Avalon and all the good improvements which have gone into the development of this property."

When William Wrigley Jr. purchased the property, it was, to quote one Avalon merchant, "Catalina Island's rediscovery." New policies in business and local government were adopted. Reorganization in administration was necessary, but many of the old employees who had been years in the service of the Banning Brothers, retained their employment. Fired with the "Wrigley enthusiasm", local employees sincerely sought to adapt themselves to the eastern business methods.

THE NEW AVALON

Old buildings began to disappear and new ones were erected. Streets were torn up for sewers, water mains, gas lines and other public utilities. New steamers and piers were built for the cross-channel equipment to and from the mainland. Old glass-bottom boats and other sea craft were sent to the "bone-yard", to be replaced by models of greater speed, safety and efficiency. Steam shovels for mining and road work appeared miraculously. Better streets, more comfortable homes for employees, cheaper food products, adequate entertainment and hotel accommodations for vis-

19

The Banning home at the Isthmus, where William Wrigley Jr. and Captain William Banning are said to have signed the agreement for the sale of the island and the SCI Company.

The living room of the Banning House. The patio just outside the window is where Mr. Banning and Mr. William Wrigley Jr. may have signed the papers changing ownership of the island.

Window views from the Banning home overlooking Isthmus. Left, is looking out one of the sunroom windows, and right, is a view from the living room.

The *Catalina Islander* (local Catalina newspaper) ran this story, dated February 25, 1919.

"*Control of Santa Catalina Island, world famous playground and mecca of deep-sea fishermen, on Tuesday formally passed from the hands of the Banning interests to William Wrigley Jr. The papers were signed at the office of Blankenhorn-Hunter Company in the Trust Savings Bank Building by Captain William Banning for the Banning interests and by Mr. Wrigley, says the L.A. Times.*"

William standing in front of his home on Mt. Ada in Avalon, lighting up his ever-present cigar.

"William Wrigley Jr., American."
In 1933, "he was the last of those
super-salesmen, super-showmen,
super-self-made men."
— Fortune Magazine

In the latter part of 1919, Mr. Wrigley bought out his partners in order to develop the island in his own way, not simply as a real estate venture aimed at making a quick profit.

"There is to be nothing of the Coney Island flavor about Santa Catalina." he said. "It would be unthinkable to mar the beauty of such a spot with roller coasters and the like."

According to Wrigley's biographer, William Zimmerman, Wrigley said his reason for developing Catalina was "to put within reach for the rank and file of the United States – the people to whom I owe my prosperity – a playground where they can enjoy themselves to the utmost, at such a reasonable figure of expense that all can participate in its benefits."

In a major profile, *Fortune* magazine wrote that in 1919, "Catalina was (already) a resort, but nowhere big and booming enough for Wrigley's taste." With his usual energy, Wrigley immediately began a wide range of projects to improve on and expand the resort concepts the Bannings had begun.

One of the first major projects completed was the construction of the Hotel Atwater, named in honor of Wrigley's daughter-in-law, Helen Atwater Wrigley. Built in several months under difficult conditions, it was ready just in time for the summer season of 1920.

That year, Wilmington Transportation Company's 265-foot, 1,625-passenger steamer the *SS Avalon* had gone into service. The same year, a new passenger and freight terminal was completed in Wilmington. Four years later, the 308-foot, 1,963-passenger ship *SS Catalina* was added to the cross-channel service.

The Hotel Atwater, named after William Wrigley Jr.'s daughter-in-law Helen Atwater Wrigley.

1921 was another busy year for Catalina. Mr. Wrigley's Chicago Cubs baseball team began making annual spring training visits to Avalon. They continued interrupted only by World War II, for thirty years.

Between March and September of 1921, a beautiful home was built for Mr. and Mrs. Wrigley on their ridge-top property at the southeast edge of Avalon. D.M. Renton and draftsman Walter Harris designed Mount Ada, named for Wrigley's wife. From an elevation of over three hundred and fifty feet, the house overlooks Avalon Canyon, including Avalon Bay and the area where the Cubs' spring training camp was located.

In the mid-1920s, Catalina remained a hive of activity. In 1923, with the laying of 23 miles of undersea cable, the island was finally fully connected to the mainland by telephone service. In 1924, a long-standing problem of a lack of fresh water was eased considerably by the construction of the Thompson Dam, which created a reservoir in Middle Canyon.

William Wrigley Jr. and D.M. Renton.

Thompson Reservoir was created to supply fresh water to the residents of Catalina.

After spending some time on the island, Mr. Wrigley could clearly see that school facilities needed room to grow. He donated six acres of land in Falls Canyon, on which both an elementary and a high school were built in 1925. That same year, Mrs. Ada Wrigley donated the Deagan Chimes to the community. They were placed on the mountain above the future location of the Casino, as a symbol of her love for Avalon and her generosity. Today these chimes still ring out for all to enjoy.

Two premier attractions created under the supervision of William Wrigley Jr., were the Bird Park, which opened in 1928; and the Casino, with its theater and ballroom, which had its gala opening the following year.

As a testament to Wrigley's vision for Catalina, tourist visits to the island increased from 90,000 to 750,000 between 1919 and 1929 – an increase of 833 percent. That kind of success came as a result of sound planning that made people's vacation experiences, whether they stayed one day or one month, pleasant and memorable.

"Catalina Island is the playground for all, rich or poor, youth or aged." he said in 1920. *"All classes mix with democratic spirit."*

His descendants, son Philip, grandson Bill, great-grandson Paxson and great-granddaughter Alison honor that philosophy.

The Bird Park was a wonderful attraction and a memorable visit by early travelers to Catalina. The 90 foot diameter steel cage was built in 1928 and no admission was charged to enter the 7-1/2 acre park.

The Deagan Chimes donated to the community by Mrs. Ada Wrigley in 1925 at a cost of $25,000.

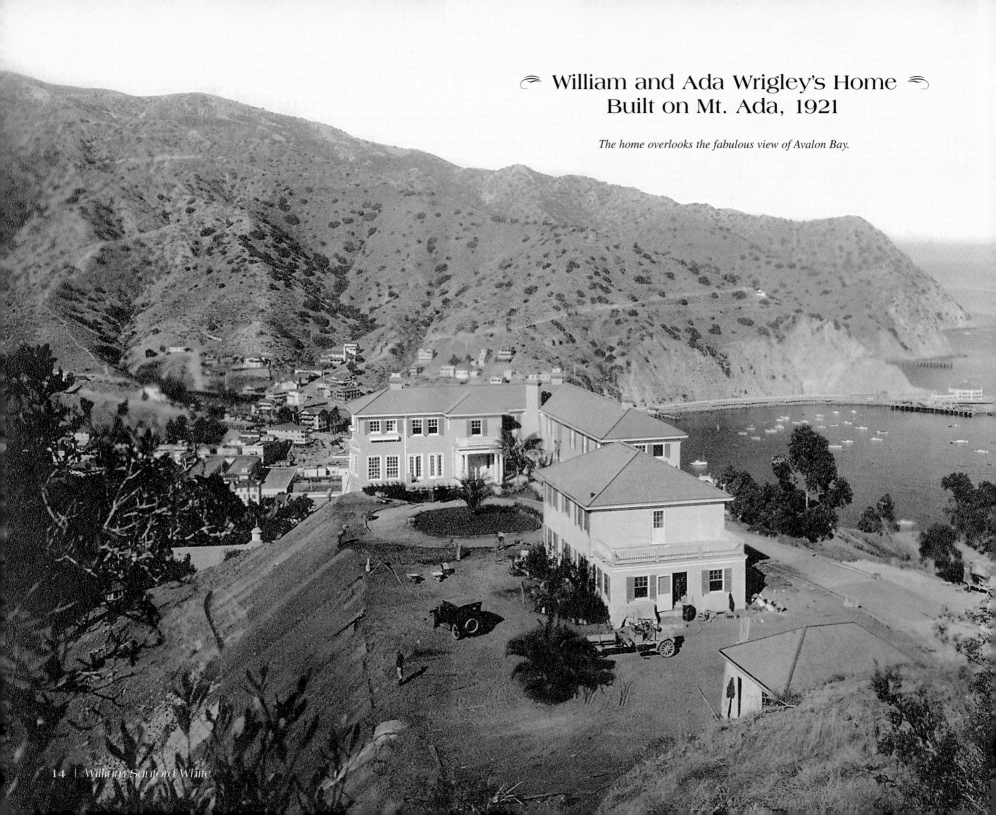

❧ William and Ada Wrigley's Home ❧
Built on Mt. Ada, 1921

The home overlooks the fabulous view of Avalon Bay.

Green Gables, the Wrigley home in Lake Geneva, Wisconsin.

This Wrigley home, on the hill in the foreground, overlooks the Arizona Biltmore in Phoenix. It is now known as The Wrigley Mansion Club. This photo was taken circa 1926-1927.

Joining an impressive array of Wrigley homes in Chicago; Lake Geneva in Wisconsin; Pasadena, California; and Phoenix, Arizona, Mount Ada rose high on the mountainside south of Avalon. The main house is L-shaped, with a second-story bridge connecting to a large wing running parallel to the drive. There are several smaller outlying buildings on the grounds. The landscape has evolved over the years, it features oleander and lantana plants as well as eucalyptus, palm, and pepper trees. The ridge-top location enjoys a constant breeze, keeping bothersome insects to a minimum. Lofty Mount Ada catches the first golden rays of each sunrise, and the last crimson beams of sunset.

Above, William and Ada's home during construction. Below, the completed home with hillsides graded and ready for landscaping.

Entry stairway and hall at Mt. Ada home in Avalon.

Dining room overlooking Avalon Bay and Lover's Cove.

Pool table and recreation room at Mt. Ada.

William Wrigley Jr.'s home office.

View of Avalon Bay from living room of Mt. Ada home.

Living room and fireplace at Mt. Ada home.

Interior photos of the Wrigley home on Mt. Ada

Mt. Ada guest bedroom.

Living room at Mt. Ada.

The Sunroom has a view of both Avalon Canyon and Avalon Bay.

Sitting room for Mrs. Wrigley.

View of Avalon Canyon and Cubs Training Field.

William Wrigley Jr.'s desk at Mt. Ada home.

Exterior views of classic Georgian Colonial home built in 1921 by Mr. and Mrs. William Wrigley Jr.

Wilmington Transportation Company

A key element of William Wrigley Jr.'s, development of Catalina was the Wilmington Transportation Company (WTCo). In 1887, early island owner George Shatto had selected WTCo to provide both freight and passenger service from San Pedro to Catalina Island. At first, passengers were carried on tugboats, but as business grew, two small passenger steamers, the *Warrior* and the *Falcon*, were put into service. When the Banning brothers purchased Santa Catalina and incorporated as the Santa Catalina Island Company, they deeded the WTCo to the new corporation.

When the cash-strapped Banning brothers sold the Santa Catalina Island Company to Mr. Wrigley in 1919, the sale included the passenger vessels, tugs and barges of the WTCo. While they have been two distinct companies since their creation in the 19th century, their activities were strongly linked. Operating the transportation company in tandem with the Santa Catalina Island Company allowed Mr. Wrigley to tackle almost any project independently.

Pacific Electric Red Street Car waiting at the foot of Avalon Boulevard in Wilmington near the steamer terminal for passengers to be transported to downtown Los Angeles.

Catalina Island Steamer Terminal, Wilmington, where all the Wrigley ships moored for passengers and freight service, 1935. Shown above is the steamship SS Catalina.

WTCo passenger vessels steamed to the island loaded with tourists who stayed at Santa Catalina Island Company hotels and tent cabins. Those ships would pass WTCo barges crossing the channel loaded with rock from quarries at Empire Landing and near Pebbly Beach. The light-colored volcanic Catalina rock, known as felsite, was used to create the breakwaters at Long Beach, Santa Barbara and Port Hueneme-Oxnard.

Mr. Wrigley purchased a passenger steamer, the *S.S. Virginia*, from the Goodrich Steamship line and had it refurbished and renamed the *S.S. Avalon*. Next, he commissioned the *S.S. Catalina*, built by the Los Angeles Shipbuilding and Drydock Company and launched in 1924. The *S.S. Catalina* measured 301 feet in length and had a beam of 52 feet.

S.S. Avalon *at Steamer Pier in Avalon in 1920.*

This brand new Wilmington Transportation car was being hoisted aboard a steamer headed for Catalina. It seems to have slipped, on the berth at the Los Angeles Harbor.

Guests aboard the S.S. Cabrillo *in 1920.*

Tourists and guests disembarking from the S.S. Catalina *in Avalon always enjoyed a huge reception from residents and other guests on the island. Everyone felt important and welcomed.*

The S.S. Avalon *pulling into Avalon Bay.*

WTCo Tugboat was used to pull S.S. Avalon *away from mainland dock before heading to open sea.*

The vessel was originally licensed to carry 1,950 passengers. With safety refinements, the total was later raised to 2,200. The *S.S. Catalina* was christened by Miss Marcia Patrick, daughter of Joseph Patrick, president of the SCI Company, on May 3, 1924. According to Lester Glenn Arellanes, the *S.S. Catalina* was the last honest-to-goodness steamship of her kind under United States Registry. Also launched in 1924 were the tour boats the *Blanche W*, named after William Wrigley Jr.'s only grandchild at the time, Ada Blanche Wrigley, and the glass bottom boat, *Princess*.

Built in 1904, the S.S. Cabrillo *was abandoned near Sacramento, California after being used as a WW II Troop transporter.*

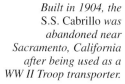

Couriers aboard S.S. Catalina.

S.S. Cabrillo *docked in Avalon Bay.*

From 1919 into the 1930s, 1940s and beyond, the Wrigleys and their associates conducted the operations of both the WTCo and the Santa Catalina Island Company. In the early 1920s, Mr. Wrigley developed a "day trip" concept for Catalina. Visitors from the mainland could come to Catalina for the day and participate in all the free activities and attractions for the cost of a round-trip steamer ticket. This concept was so successful that visitors to the island increased from 90,000 in 1919 to 750,000 in 1930.

S.S. Catalina *tied to Steamer Pier in Avalon Bay, 1930s.*

⌒ Hotels ⌒
& Residential Housing

During its glory years, the Hotel St. Catherine consisted of a long, four-story main building, a wing nearly the same size, tennis courts, a swimming pool, and a banquet room that could seat a thousand.

The Hotel Atwater on Sumner Avenue was built in 1920. The right wing was never completed. Plans changed, eliminating upstairs rooms to make space for the world's largest cafeteria, which was operated by the SCI Co. for only two years. The space was later converted into the present day arcade and Post Office.

Hotel St. Catherine in Descanso Bay, Avalon, California.

Hotel Atwater in Avalon was built in 1920 and was open for business in six months after construction began. It was named in honor of Wrigley's daughter-in-law, Helen Atwater.

Over a thousand people could be seated in the Banquet Room, inside the Hotel St. Catherine in Avalon.

The Hotel St. Catherine's swimming pool.

Descanso Avenue private housing for residents.

The Island Villas offered island guests efficient accommodations.

Sumner Avenue.

Many cottage homes were built in Avalon between 1920-1921, including those on Lower Descanso Avenue. The Santa Catalina Island Company sold fee title to individual property owners for a total price of approximately $500.

When William Wrigley Jr. assumed ownership of the Island, he was troubled by the poor living conditions of the Mexican community. Tremont Street became the site for a small community of buildings reminiscent of a typical Mexican village. Shacks were torn down and replaced with white stucco, tile-roofed buildings featuring three and four family apartments, that rented for $10 to $15 per month. Twelve bachelor apartments were also built, and rented for $4 a month.

View from the hills overlooking Tremont Street during construction.

Children playing in the neighborhood of the Tremont Street homes.

~ Tourism ~
& Business Development

The early business developments of William Wrigley Jr. were numerous and varied. They included the Catalina Country Club, with an expanded golf course, ranching, mining, pottery and tiles, island hunting, tourism and excursions.

During the early 1920s, the Catalina Furniture Factory milled lumber for most of the island's buildings and furniture. The rough wood was barged to Avalon and then moved to the factory, which was located across from the Bird Park.

The Tuna Club, founded in 1898, had a number of famous honorary members including Calvin Coolidge, Herbert Hoover, and William Wrigley Jr. It is still active in the Avalon community today.

The Catalina Country Club was expanded to offer 18-holes under William Wrigley Jr.

Sightseeing Jaunting Cars were brought to Catalina by Wrigley to expand tourist activities throughout the island.

Today, the Tuna Club looks much as it did when originally built in 1898. The original structure was destroyed during the 1915 fire.

Flying fish tours became a very popular activity for visitors with the lauch of the Blanche W. flying fish boat.

FLYING FISH, CATALINA ISLAND, CALIF.

By the turn of the century, a glass-bottom boat tour was one of the island's "musts." Visitors could view the splendor beneath the waves – the swaying kelp gardens, the bright orange garibaldi fish, and the deep sea divers – all without getting wet.

In 1927, the manufacturing of brick and roof tiles began at a newly created plant in Pebbly Beach. The new business contributed to the economy of Catalina Island. The Catalina Tile Company recruited many talented ceramic artisans and production workers to design the new lines of decorative tile and pottery. During the peak production years, between 10,000 and 15,000 pieces were produced per week in kilns heated with fuel oil. Today, Catalina tile and pottery are in great demand with collectors and command high prices.

Guests viewing the underwater gardens in glass bottom boats in Avalon Bay.

The Catalina Island Yacht Club, built in 1925, continues to offer the community and members a place for social activities as well as participating in community service. This was the original site of the Meteor Boat Co. in 1914

Catalina tile and pottery was displayed and sold in this Crescent Avenue shop in Avalon.

Pebbly Beach Catalina Pottery and Tile Manufacturing Plant.

Today Catalina Pottery and Tile are considered highly collectable.

Heywood's Department Store, located under the Glenmore Hotel, allowed residents to shop for a wide selection of items without having to travel to the mainland.

Cattle ranching was popular on the island. Cattle were herded into large corrals on the beach at the Isthmus to await transport.

The mid-1920s brought a flurry of mining activity to Catalina. Renton Mine in the mountains behind Pebbly Beach and another mine on Mount Black Jack generated ore for a short time. The ore was processed at the Silver Isle 100-Ton floatation Mill at White's Landing. Silver, zinc, and lead were extracted for about two years before the operation slowed due to dwindling yields.

Poultry and pig ranches in Avalon Canyon provided islanders with fresh meat for many years.

Silver Isle 100-Ton Floatation Mill at White's Landing. 500 cloth sacks filled with 150 pounds each of zinc concentrate were shipped directly to Belgium every two weeks. All ore from Renton and Black Jack Mines was processed at this mill during the 1920s.

Orange groves were located in Avalon Canyon prior to the development of the Chicago Cubs Spring Training Camp.

Sporting Events & Entertainment

In 1921, William Wrigley Jr. brought the Chicago Cubs to Avalon for spring training. Between 1921 and 1951 the Cubs came to Avalon each year, except for the war years, when the island was given over to military activities. The Cubs were a Wrigley team, and in the small town of Avalon the Wrigleys were friends and benefactors to just about everyone. Avalon opened its hearts and doors to the players making it a magical time for the island and the team.

J.H. Patrick, Joe McCarthy, J. LeLivelt, William Wrigley Jr.

Philip, center, and his wife Helen, far left, observe filming of Cubs Spring Training highlights.

Cubs enjoying a leisurely row in Avalon Bay.

William Wrigley Jr. greets Commissioner of Baseball Kenesaw Mountain Landis at the Steamer Pier, 1930.

William Wrigley Jr. built an impressive practice field in Avalon Canyon.

William Wrigley, Jr., center, surrounded by his beloved Chicago Cubs.

In the Wrigley Ocean Marathon of 1927, over one hundred entrants, including many famous swimmers from around the world, plunged into the channel at Two Harbors to swim to the mainland. A rowboat accompanied each contestant, and a small fleet of powerboats remained close at hand. As darkness came, dozens of swimmers had already been helped out of the water. Early in the morning on the following day, in front of thousands of people, George Young of Toronto, Canada, was the only person to finish the race.

Mr. Wrigley and Joseph H. Patrick with jumbo-sized version of marathon winner's check for $25,000.

In 1927 swimmers from around the globe came to compete in the Wrigley Marathon. Swimmers swam from the Isthmus to San Pedro on the mainland. The winning prize of $25,000 went to 17-year-old George Young from Canada.

Toward the end of William Wrigley Jr.'s first decade as patron of the island, he felt the need for a grand achievement to crown his achievements on Catalina. And so the idea for a Casino was born. It would be a dance pavilion, assembly hall and theater, built on the small peninsula between Avalon and Descanso bays known as Sugarloaf Point.

Standing 140 feet high, measuring 178 feet in diameter, the Avalon Casino has an exterior gallery that encircles the structure at the 75 foot level. The main entrance on the landward side of the building features a magnificent tiled mosaic, a recreation of Botticelli's *The Birth of Venus*. The theater foyer is 20 feet wide and 160 feet long, following the building's curvature. It is lined on both inside walls with panels of black walnut. The theater's 40-foot-high ceiling and walls are adorned with nine mural panels, each 10 feet wide and 20 feet high. The theater was the first in the world designed to present "talkies," or motion pictures with vocal sound tracks. The Casino has three levels – the theater level, a mezzanine, and above that the ballroom. The Casino's revolutionary use of open space inspired architects and engineers around the country, including designers from New York City who later constructed Radio City Music Hall.

The original Sugarloaf Casino built by William Wrigley Jr. in 1920.

Dancers filled the Casino Ballroom, the world's largest circular ballroom, throughout the 1930s and 1940s.

Murals by John Gabriel Beckman grace the interior of the Casino's movie theater.

In 1930, the architect and design firm Weber & Spaulding were presented the Honor Award for the cantilevered design of Wrigley's Casino.

Final stages of construction of the Sugarloaf Casino.

The Avalon Music Bowl.

In the 1930s, the lineup of big bands at the Casino's ballroom was always top-notch. Many bands arrived around mid June and stayed the entire summer. Bands also performed at the Bandbox Theater, the St. Catherine Hotel, and several of the other larger hotels. Musical plays were staged at the Riviera Theater at Crescent and Clarissa Avenues as well as at the Avalon Theater and the Bird Park.

Early Catalina Island resort brochures.

Wrigley's development of Avalon continued to provide varied entertainment choices for residents and visitors alike.

In its heyday, the Bird Park covered a full eight acres and held 500 cages of varying sizes displaying 8,000 birds from around the world. The huge birdcage was created from the dome-shaped roof supports of the old dance pavilion, which was removed for construction of the Casino. It became the world's largest single birdcage.

The Annual Tug Of War in Avalon Bay continued into the Wrigley era.

Wrigley's Bird Park was a tourist destination in Avalon until mid 1966 when the birds were relocated to the new Los Angeles Zoo.

Eagle's Nest, Catalina Island

Tourists rode stagecoaches and buses throughout the interior of the island, stopping at the Eagle's Nest for rest and refreshment.

Education & Public Utilities

During the spring of 1919, the Pacific Telephone and Telegraph Company installed the first commercial radio telephone system at Pebbly Beach, with a sister station at San Pedro. In 1921, a local telephone exchange was installed in Avalon with seventy-five subscribers. In 1923, because many radio receivers could listen in on island-to-mainland conversations, the telephone company built an office on Whittley Avenue and laid two submarine cables to the mainland.

The Telephone Company building on Whittley Avenue was built in 1923 by the Pacific Telephone & Telegraph Company. At left is telephone man Ralph Brown standing next to manager (Judge) Ernest Windle.

Catalina was connected to the mainland by a 23-mile undersea telephone cable in 1923 when US Army cableship S.S. Dellwood installed the communication system.

The Wrigley Family was committed to providing education to the residents of Avalon throughout the years. In 1925, an elementary and high school were built on 6 acres of land in Falls Canyon donated by William Wrigley Jr.

D.M. Renton recalled the gigantic task of creating a water storage and transport system for the island. "Water was one of the first major developments for Catalina. Tunnels were dug, springs developed, wells drilled, pipelines installed, and finally a series of dams and reservoirs constructed including the large 100 million gallon dam at Middle Ranch. The water problem was not the only one that had to be licked. There was a new sewer system, gas plant and mains, diesel electric power plants, mountain roads, sight-seeing bus operations, hotels and villa accommodations."

In his book, "Windle's History of Santa Catalina Island" Ernest Windle wrote that "...no municipality could have brought the Catalina water system to its present efficiency without a bonded indebtedness of more than three million dollars. As one of his philanthropic acts, Mr. Wrigley not only donated the money to pay for the unique water system, but he furnished the equipment and employed men with an enthusiasm for solving difficult problems."

New Falls Canyon Avalon School built in 1925 on land donated by William Wrigley Jr.

Thompson Reservoir was created for fresh water. Below, the new spillway being created.

Santo Catalina Island Company Managers & Administrators

Joseph H. Patrick, David M. Renton and John Windle accompanied William Wrigley Jr. in 1927 on the day the decision was made on the location of the new dance pavilion.

Patrick had been a friend and associate of William Wrigley Jr. prior to Wrigley's purchase of Catalina Island. He was elected to key positions in the Wrigley corporations, including president of both the Santa Catalina Island Company (SCI) and the Wilmington Transportation Company, and after April 1932 was chairman of SCI Company.

Joseph H. Patrick.

Judge Ernest Windle (seated), Mayor Wilbur Lee White (Standing), 1966.

William Wrigley, Jr. and D.M. Renton at the Catalina Country Club.

Between 1919 and 1932, William Wrigley Jr. and David M. Renton planned and carried out dozens of projects on Santa Catalina Island, including the construction of the Casino, the homes of William and Philip K. Wrigley, the Catalina Airport at Hamilton Beach, the Atwater Hotel, the Country Club with an improved golf course, the Sunshine Terrace development, and the William Wrigley Jr. Memorial. His son, Malcolm J. Renton, also worked on Catalina, starting out as an assistant to his father, later becoming the assistant to Philip K. Wrigley, and eventually attaining the position of senior vice president, director and corporate secretary for the Santa Catalina Island Company.

Judge Ernest Windle, a magistrate of the Santa Catalina-San Clemente Island Justice Court, accompanied William Wrigley Jr. on his initial inspection tour of Santa Catalina Island and notarized the bill of sale by the Bannings. His son John W.R. Windle went to work as a messenger boy for the Santa Catalina Island Company when he was sixteen. Soon he was promoted to truck driver, and after a number of years was made superintendent of transportation. John Windle was an employee of the SCI Company for 31 years.

Celebrated Residents & Famous Visitors – Presidents & Dignitaries

William Wrigley Jr. welcomed Calvin Coolidge, Herbert Hoover, the Prince of Wales, and many other prominent guests to Avalon in the ten years the Wrigleys spent their vacations at Mount Ada.

From the 1920s on, a "Who's Who" of prominent people vacationed at Avalon or Two Harbors, anchoring their pleasure craft in one of the many sheltered coves along Catalina's leeward coast. From the film industry, the list includes film directors John Ford, Howard Hawks, and Orson Welles, as well as actors John Barrymore, Jean Harlow, Lawrence Olivier, Clark Gable, Humphrey Bogart, David Niven, Henry Fonda, Errol Flynn, John Wayne, Judy Garland, Charlie Chaplin, Paulette Goddard, Mickey Rooney, Stan Laurel, and Oliver Hardy.

President Calvin Coolidge visits with William Wrigley Jr. in the garden at Mt. Ada.

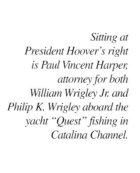

A 188 pound marlin caught by Sir Winston Churchill at Catalina Island, posing here with Captain Monte Foster and Ben R. Meyer, prominent Los Angeles banker, circa 1929.

Sitting at President Hoover's right is Paul Vincent Harper, attorney for both William Wrigley Jr. and Philip K. Wrigley aboard the yacht "Quest" fishing in Catalina Channel.

The biggest names in music came to Avalon, including Benny Goodman, Bing Crosby, Kay Kyser, and Perry Como. Dozens of the most popular big bands in the nation played at Avalon Casino through the 1930s and into the 1940s. Among these were Curt Houck and his Orchestra, the Jan Garber Orchestra, and the bands of Freddy Martin, Dick Jurgens, Buddy Rogers, and (Bing's brother) Bob Crosby.

Avalon homeowners of the 1920s and 1930s included authors Zane Grey and Gene Stratton Porter as well as cowboy star Tom Mix. The young woman who later assumed the stage name of Marilyn Monroe also lived for a time at Avalon in the early 1940s, while her husband trained with the Merchant Marine.

Political figures, like everyone else, tend to fall under Catalina's spell. Since 1919, many U.S. Presidents have come to the island. Calvin Coolidge, Herbert Hoover, Richard Nixon and Ronald Reagan all visited. In August of 1923, Warren G. Harding was scheduled to stop in Avalon during a west coast tour, but he fell ill and died in San Francisco just a few days earlier. Mr. Reagan, who in the 1930s, worked as a radio announcer for Chicago Cubs baseball, made three spring training trips to Avalon with the team, 1935 through 1937. Winston Churchill, who enjoyed sportfishing, tried the waters off Catalina.

Filming of the 1935 version of Mutiny On The Bounty, starring Clark Gable, took place at the Isthmus.

The "King of Catalina" and the SeaHawk, during filming at the Isthmus.

Director Irving Thalberg, and stars Norma Shearer, Paulette Goddard and Charlie Chaplin aboard the yacht Invader.

Legendary early cowboy Tom Mix, owned a home on Maiden Lane in Avalon.

Comedian Oliver Hardy ready to tee off from Guy Kibbe's head at the Golf Club.

Hardy substituting a tennis ball for a golf ball at the Catalina Visitors Golf Club.

Band Leader Jan Garber congratulates Mrs. Stan Laurel and husband for catching a marlin.

The American Indian style adobe home built by Zane Grey in 1924 overlooks Avalon Bay.

Author and sportsman Zane Grey with his wife, Dolly.

⤛ Dr. Julia Strawn ⤜

Over a period of many years, one of Ada Wrigley's closest friends was Dr. Julia Strawn. She had attended medical school in the 1890s, a time when men far outnumbered women in the field of medicine. Her specialties were surgery and homeopathic medicine, and her skills were of tremendous help to the family on a number of occasions.

She traveled widely with the Wrigleys, including trips to Catalina. Around 1902, she performed an emergency appendectomy on eight year-old Philip. Emergency operations of that kind were not altogether unusual early in the 20th century, but this operation took place on the Wrigley kitchen table. Dr. Strawn accompanied William Jr. and Ada Wrigley, young Philip, and his sister Dorothy on an around-the-world tour in 1913. In the years that followed she delivered all three of Philip and Helen Wrigley's children.

Three generations of Wrigleys trusted her as a physician, and regarded her as a sort of adopted aunt they affectionately called "Dockie."

Dr. Julia Strawn, known to the Wrigleys as "Dockie."

Philip K. Wrigley
Born 1894 – Died 1977
The Legacy Remains

ISLAND ACHIEVEMENTS – 1925 to 1977

Purchased Home at Casa del Monte in Avalon

Established Arabian Horse Ranch El Rancho Escondido

Transportation

Began Wilmington-Catalina Airline Passenger Service

Hamilton Cove Airport for Amphibious Passenger Planes

Airport-in-the-Sky Landing Field & Terminal

Scheduled Passenger Service by United Airlines

Road Built Between El Rancho Escondido & Airport

Sale of Cross-Channel Steamships

Avalon Steamer Pier Dismantled

Residential Housing, Infrastructure & Public Utilities

Sold Land & Constructed Homes for Local Residents

Opened Multiple-Unit Housing at Hamilton Cove, Canyon Terrace,
  Sol Vista & Fairview

Transfer of Public Utility Service to Southern California Edison Company

Avalon & Island Streets & Roads Paved & Improved

Island Landmarks

Redesigned Front Street Crescent Avenue
  (Serpentine seawall, fountains, tile benches, olive & palm trees)

Opened El Encanto Building & Plaza

Constructed William Wrigley Jr. Memorial & Gardens

Removed Island Villas, Bird Park & St. Catherine Hotel

**Conversion from Tourist Resort to World War II Wartime
  Fortification & Training**

US Maritime, Coast Guard, US Army Signal Corps

OSS (Central Intelligence Agency)

Transition from World War II to Peacetime

Entertainment

Casino Point Diving Bell

Hotel St. Catherine Replaced by Descanso Beach Recreation Center

Expanded Seasonal Excursions & Travel Business

Continued Chicago Cubs Spring Training

Established All-Women Baseball League "League Of Their Own"

Casino Ballroom – Started National Radio Broadcasts

Redecorated Casino Ballroom as Nightclub Setting
  (tables, chairs, food service)

Converted Golf Course to 9-holes for Privately Owned Hotel Development

Established Catalina Island Conservancy and USC Marine Institute

PART TWO
PHILIP KNIGHT WRIGLEY
THE LEGACY REMAINS

*"In Everything He Did, Phil Wrigley
Demonstrated An Incorruptible Integrity"*
Don Kowet, Chicago Magazine, 1977

Philip Knight Wrigley was born December 5, 1894, to Ada Elizabeth and William Wrigley Jr. Growing up, Philip traveled widely with his family, both in the United States and abroad. An around-the-world tour at the close of his teenage years took him to Hawaii, Hong Kong, Indonesia, India, Egypt and more. He continued to travel with his family throughout his life.

Philip was very interested in the historical aspects of the places he visited. When he and his wife, Helen visited India, Mrs. Wrigley found a travel guide to lecture on some of the interesting things to see in the area. The guide was describing a beautiful set of spire-like towers out in the country when Philip entered their room. Without having heard the previous conversation, he said "Oh, those must be the Towers of Silence…" and went on to talk in detail about the Hindu burial site. The guide was astounded that Philip knew the history and location of this sacred place.

When he was twenty, Philip sailed for Australia, where he spent nearly a year managing the Wrigley chewing gum operation there. It was an active, "hands-on" job, far better to his mind than sitting in a prep school classroom, where he had found some academic subjects tedious.

Chief Warrant Officer Philip K. Wrigley, United States Navy 1917.

Philip in Egypt during his first world trip.

Philip K. Wrigley, kneeling front row left, training at Great Lakes 1917.

USNR Lt. JG Philip K. Wrigley 1921.

Philip replacing whistle on boat in Lake Geneva.

On June 28, 1917, as the United States was entering World War I, Philip Wrigley went on active duty with the US Naval Reserve. He served most of his hitch at the Great Lakes Naval Training Station, and his abilities became so important to that facility that he rose quickly to the rank of chief warrant officer, later gaining the post of Head of Training for aviation mechanics. In July 1921, he was honorably discharged with the rank of Lieutenant Jr. Grade.

Before long, he was back at Santa Catalina Island, where he dove eagerly into a variety of projects. Philip was deeply involved in the development of Santa Catalina long before his father's passing. As early as 1920, within months of his first visit to the island, he had been involved in land sales and construction of residential units in Avalon. All through the 1920s, he had been a key player in many projects in Avalon and around the island, including the construction of the Casino. The island benefited tremendously from his "can-do" attitude – in fact, daughter Blanny recalls that her father's favorite saying was "It can be done!" This homily appeared on a plaque in Philip's office, and he referred to it often.

Catalina Tile and Pottery Plant in Pebbly Beach.

Cabin Cruiser "Wasp" was transported from Lake Michigan to Catalina Island, Hamilton Cove Airport.

Casa Del Monte in Avalon, the home of Philip K. Wrigley and his family.

Philip oversaw the construction of the brickyard and tile plant at Pebbly Beach as well as the furniture-making facility and lumber mill in Avalon Canyon across from the Bird Park. He was also involved in the 1922 construction of the dance pavilion on Sugarloaf Point – the precursor to the 1929 Casino built by his father.

In the years after he became a Wrigley Company executive, Philip could afford to live anywhere, and had several residences, both for work and relaxation. But like his father, he had a deep love for Santa Catalina Island. So in 1927, when his daughters Ada Blanche (nicknamed Blanny) and Dorothy (nicknamed Deedie) were four and two respectively, he and his wife purchased an island home, Casa del Monte, in Avalon. They and their children spent many happy times in this lovely hillside home. Their third child, William, was born in 1933.

Backyard view of Casa Del Monte overlooking Avalon Bay.

Clockwise from top: Deedie, Blanny and Bill Wrigley at Casa del Monte.

Philip and Helen's children, Blanny left, Deedie, right, and little William, "Billy."

Philip and Helen Wrigley wanted their children to look upon the fame of the Wrigley business interests, and the wealth of the Wrigley family with a clear eye. They wanted them to understand money – the earning, the spending, and the saving of it.

The close attention the couple devoted to these things was one of the central themes of Arthur Meyerhoff's book on Philip Wrigley. Meyerhoff, owner of an advertising agency, had a 44 year professional and social relationship with Philip. After his friend passed on in 1977, Meyerhoff wrote a memoir – a tribute, really. It was titled *The Personality and Principles of Philip K. Wrigley*. Reportedly, copies were given to those closest to Philip, including his three children, Blanny, Deedie, and Bill.

Meyerhoff wrote, "Philip Wrigley gave two rare gifts to his children: self-sufficiency and balance. (He) was the type of parent who was aware of those…often insidious effects of inherited wealth and a famous family name."

Meyerhoff also quotes a letter young Philip wrote to his father that distinctly shows Philip's characteristics of honesty and clear thinking. "I have always considered being the son of a prominent man more of a disadvantage than an advantage," he wrote. "That is why I have always wanted people to get to know me first, and then find out who I am."

Philip was not being ironic in referring to that "disadvantage." He had observed too many spoiled rich kids, and knew what he said was true. Meyerhoff also sums up the life lesson on confidence that Philip learned from William Wrigley Jr., and passed on to his son and daughters: "As soon as you trust yourself, you will know how to live."

Despite being born into great wealth, all three of these Wrigley children were, in the words of Meyerhoff, "intelligent, successful, and thoroughly decent individuals."

Blanny, Deedie, and Bill all had chores and other responsibilities from a young age. They understood what it meant to clean out a barn, and they understood how to balance "cash on hand" and expenditures. The story was passed among family friends that, at age ten, Blanny carried her own checkbook, and routinely wrote checks for her purchases at the stores of Avalon.

Arthur Meyerhoff, Vice President in charge of marketing, Wm Wrigley Jr. Gum Company.

As an adult, Philip's daughter Blanny recalled the lessons of self-reliance that were taught to her in childhood: "Our parents wanted us to understand that we were normal American citizens, not members of some privileged class." Blanny recalls that at an early age all the children were expected to perform daily home duties to reinforce this principle. At El Rancho Escondido, her chore each morning was to make her own bed and clean and refill all the kerosene lamps in the ranch house, making sure that she trimmed the wicks.

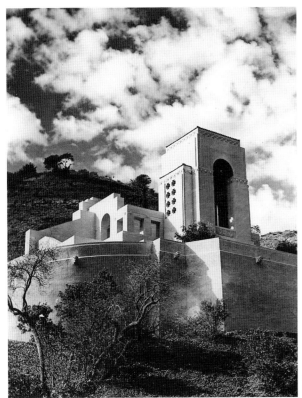

When William Wrigley Jr., passed away early in 1932, Philip Wrigley became the central figure in the planning of innovations at Catalina.

As a tribute to the legacy William Wrigley Jr. left to Santa Catalina Island, Philip and his mother Ada oversaw the design and construction of the Wrigley Mausoleum, Memorial, and Botanical Gardens at the head of picturesque Avalon Canyon. The monument is a fitting tribute to a great humanitarian, businessman, and family patriarch. Construction of the Mausoleum began in July 1933. The main tower is 80 feet high and includes beautiful Catalina tiles made on the island.

In 1946, Philip had his father's remains moved from the mausoleum to Forest Lawn Cemetery in Glendale, California where they are interred today.

The Botanical Gardens are the perfect place to become familiar with the island's plant life. They were merged with the Catalina Island Conservancy in 1996 and are a popular island destination today.

Wrigley Mausoleum, Memorial, and Botanical Gardens in Avalon Canyon.

The Botanical Gardens in upper Avalon Canyon.

The Chicago Cubs take a moment to pose with Philip Wrigley, center, wearing his coat and tie.

Avalon city manager Earle Pollok shakes hands with pitcher Dizzy Dean when the Chicago Cubs disembark from the S.S. Catalina at the Steamer Pier in 1940. Also in attendance are Cubs manager Gabby Hartnett (left) and mayor Wilbur White.

For a short time following his father's death, Philip Wrigley did not have a controlling interest in the Chicago Cubs baseball team, although they continued to hold spring training in Avalon. He moved quickly to acquire control and became president of the Cubs organization in 1934.

The annual trips to Avalon for spring training from 1921 to 1951 were important in making the Cubs a tight-knit unit. During World War II, many of the players had been drafted, so Philip established the All Women's Baseball League, which later became the subject and theme for the movie "League Of Their Own." The women's teams never played on Catalina.

During Philip's tenure as owner, Ronald Reagan made a memorable appearance in Avalon as a sports announcer covering the Cubs at training camp from 1935-1937. Reagan made a trip to Hollywood while on the island, had a screen test at Warner Brothers, and the rest is history. At Philip's death in 1977, ownership of the Chicago team was turned over to his wife Helen. At her passing, ownership was turned over to their son, William "Bill" Wrigley.

Ernie Reyes and accompanist performed authentic Spanish Dances at the Plaza.

Inside patio of the El Encanto Plaza.

From 1932 through 1934, Philip Wrigley was instrumental in the conception, planning and construction of El Encanto Plaza, opposite the entrance to Casino Way, and refinements to Avalon's beachfront promenade, Crescent Avenue.

Entrance of El Encanto looking out onto Crescent Avenue.

Entrance to El Encanto from Crescent Avenue.

*Above, left, and right, construction of
Crescent Avenue's beachfront promenade
and the Serpentine Walk.*

Dorothy and Otis Shepard.

These improvements included a seawall, tiled store fronts, fountains, tiled benches and landscaping of the Serpentine Walk that passes many of the town's notable shops, restaurants and entertainment venues. Artists and designers Otis and Dorothy Sheppard were a driving force in helping make his vision of Avalon's curving waterfront strand, known as "Avenida de la Crescenta," a reality.

Philip and Helen Wrigley with their private DC-3 airplane named "Wasp."

Above, a grand view of the Catalina Airport.

Right, the airport patio, where guests could sit back, enjoy the afternoon and watch the seaplanes taxi in and out.

Below, a 180 degree turntable that allowed the seaplanes to be rotated for either parking in the hanger or takeoff into the sea.

Aviation played a vital role in Philip Wrigley's life on many levels. Grandson Philip Hagenah shared that Philip was one of the first men to fly across Lake Michigan during his time at the Great Lakes Naval Training Station during World War I. During the flight, the pilot had to land on the water at least once so that Philip could work on the engine which was giving them trouble. Most everyone was piloting amphibious flying boats at that time, as there were no landing strips or fields to use.

This was just a few short years after the Wright brothers made their famous maiden flight. Philip Wrigley described the plane they flew as mostly wings with a small and somewhat flimsy fuselage. There were no permanent seats for the pilots so they sat in small hammock-type seats that were difficult to stay in when trying to land on water.

In 1931 Philip was instrumental in the development of Wilmington-Catalina Airlines, a seaplane service. His most fascinating contribution was the design used to create a huge turntable to rotate planes 180 degrees after they taxied in and parked at the Hamilton Beach terminal near Avalon. They could then roll forward down the same ramp they had climbed, and enter the water in preparation for takeoff.

The Philip Wrigley Family aboard their DC-3 airplane enroute from Chicago. Left to right: Bill, Blanny, Helen, Deedie (between seats), and Philip.

Aerial view of completed Airport-in-the-Sky and United Airlines DC-3 approaching air strip for a landing in 1948.

Airport Tower.

Catalina aviation would be given another boost when Philip Wrigley had an air terminal built in the island's interior. Construction of the facility, financed by the Santa Catalina Island Co., was interrupted in 1941 by World War II, then completed in 1946. It was feared that the Japanese would attempt to use the landing strip in an attack on the west coast of California.

The original airstrip was created by leveling two mountain peaks and filling in three canyons at Buffalo Springs. "Airport-in-the-Sky" lies at an elevation of 1,602 feet – one of the highest points on the island. Leveling the mountaintops was a unique challenge, as was construction of the road from the airport to Middle Ranch junction, which runs atop a cliff known as China Wall. Philip Wrigley's drive and ingenuity brought it all about despite the engineering challenges.

United Airlines Passenger Terminal in Avalon.

Philip Wrigley's interest in aviation led to his involvement in the start-up of one of the earliest scheduled passenger airline services in the United States. In 1926, along with Allan Jackson of Standard Oil, Marshall Field III, and Edsel Ford, he founded American Airways. This company was later merged with National Air Transport and eventually absorbed into United Airlines in 1931.

After the completion of "Airport-in-the-Sky" in 1946, United Airlines established DC-3 passenger service to Catalina from the mainland. SCI Company tour buses were used to transport people to and from the United Airlines Passenger Terminal in Avalon. On October 24, 1959, the airport was opened to private aircraft.

Ribbon cutting at the grand opening ceremony of Catalina Airport.

Left to right, Philip Wrigley, Blanny, Deedie, Helen Wrigley, and Bill.

Ada Blanche (Blanny) and Dorothy (Deedie) Wrigley riding on Crescent Avenue in Avalon with their father, Philip K. Wrigley, in 1937.

William (Bill), Ada Blanche (Blanny) and Dorothy (Deedie).

By the 1930s, Philip and Helen Wrigley were the parents of three young children. In 1932, the infant son of aviator Charles Lindbergh was abducted from the family home and a ransom note was found. This notorious kidnapping became known as "the Crime of the Century." It is unknown exactly when or how, but the 20-month-old Lindbergh baby was killed while in the hands of the kidnappers.

The home of Philip and Helen Wrigley at 2466 Lakeview Avenue in Chicago, 1932.

William Wrigley Jr., and Philip in Packard roadster at Mt. Ada.

Philip and Helen Wrigley's children, Bill, Deedie, and Blanny.

Blanny Wrigley Schreiner remembers that after the Lindbergh kidnapping, the Philip Wrigley family moved, from a single-family home at 2466 Lakeview Avenue, Chicago, to a duplex on the 14th and 15th floors of a high-rise apartment building at 1500 Lakeshore Drive. One can imagine the effect of this crime on wealthy and famous families, like the Wrigleys. After watching the circus-like atmosphere of the Lindbergh case, many celebrities hired bodyguards to protect them not only from criminals, but from the press as well.

Another element of the Wrigley family's security measures was the hiring of Gus Mullineaux. Blanny described him as "a sort of bodyguard, a nice person – definitely a great, big, strong guy." Mullineaux was with the family for years, often traveling with them to Santa Catalina. He got on well with the children, but he did have one peculiarity. In his spare time, he would practice quick draws of his pistol in front of mirrors.

During this time of uncertainty, Santa Catalina Island became a haven for the Wrigley family – allowing them the opportunity to relax and experience freedom from the intrusion of the world at large. The Wrigley children found themselves in a safe place where they could play and explore without the cares they experienced at home in Chicago. Blanny reminisced about riding horses with her sister Deedie from the family ranch to Avalon to watch movies and munch popcorn at the Casino Theater, or over to Middle Ranch on Friday nights for a barbecue, Mexican music and dancing at the home of El Rancho Escondido manager Jack White. Not typical activities for overly "protected" kids from the big city.

One particularly foggy night, fully licensed 14-year-old Blanny was driving the old family Packard, which had no power brakes or power steering, down to Avalon from El Rancho Escondido. The fog was so thick that she couldn't see which way the road turned in front of her, especially with the long hood of the Packard in the way. Blanny asked Deedie, then 12, to sit on the hood of the old car and indicate which way the road turned by signaling with her right or left hand. The two girls got the car all the way down to town without a bump or scratch.

Mayor Wilbur White and his wife, Margaret (left) greet bandleader Kay Kyser and vocalist Ginny Simms.

Dick Jurgen's band in front of the Hotel St. Catherine, with the Casino in the background.

The Casino Ballroom continued to be a hub of musical activity throughout Philip Wrigley's leadership of Santa Catalina Island. In the 1930s, the lineup of bands at the Ballroom was always top-notch. Some bands arrived around mid-June and stayed the entire summer season, departing in September. Others came in early summer, played six weeks or so, then were replaced by other bands that closed out the season.

The swing dance craze of the mid- and late 1930s and 1940s dated from the Benny Goodman band's summer stay at Avalon in 1936. Each summer brought now-legendary bands to the Casino including the Jan Garber Orchestra, the Dick Jurgens Orchestra, and the bands of Freddy Martin and Kay Kyser. In 1940, with war looming, Bob Crosby and Benny Goodman appeared in Avalon with their orchestras to cheer up Casino visitors.

It was Philip Wrigley who arranged for live broadcasts of dance music from the Casino ballroom. The first was beamed from coast to coast on the evening of May 15, 1934 on the Columbia Broadcasting System (CBS). In the 1930s and 1940s, CBS, along with the National Broadcasting Company (NBC) and the Mutual Broadcasting System, regularly beamed live dance music across the country from the magic isle. During World War II, Catalina and the Casino contributed to the effort by staging entertainment for the troops stationed on the Island.

It was during the Big Band Era, in the summer of 1935, that Buddy Rogers, who was playing the Casino with his band, courted his future bride, Mary Pickford. Both were guests aboard the Wrigley yacht *Quest*. Earlier, Miss Pickford had her honeymoon, with then husband Douglas Fairbanks, Sr., aboard their yacht, at Descanso Beach.

S.S. Catalina during World War II and S.S. Cabrillo beyond. Both were used to ferry military and wartime workers across San Francisco Bay.

The U.S. Maritime Service Training Station office at the Hotel Atwater.

Following the Japanese attack on Pearl Harbor, tourist excursions to Santa Catalina were halted. Continuing a legacy of leadership by the Wrigley family to preserve the island's magical way of life, Philip Wrigley led the community in making a smooth transition from peace to wartime and back to a "golden age" again.

The military took control of the steamer ships *S.S. Catalina* and *S.S. Cabrillo* as well as the flying fish boat *Blanche W.* for use in the San Francisco Bay area during World War II. The *S.S. Avalon* was also requisitioned, but it was assigned exclusively to the Catalina-mainland run to carry military and civilian passengers and supplies beginning in 1943.

USMS Review and Parade on Wrigley Field, Avalon Canyon.

The Coast Guard issued identification cards to all Island residents. Everyone understood the need for the drastic changes, but it was a difficult time nonetheless. With tourism halted, the livelihoods of many islanders disappeared. A substantial number of Avalonites left for the mainland, where they could earn an income while contributing to the war effort.

Beginning in 1942, those who remained in Avalon and at the Isthmus struggled to adjust, socially and economically, to a different mode of life. Because tourism was not just the cornerstone but the foundation of Catalina's economy, Wrigley and other island leaders brainstormed a plan to help the Island while also supporting the country. In order to provide some income, a program was begun whereby Avalon commercial fishermen were supplied boat fuel by the government and contracted to fish for albacore. The fish would provide food for both military and civilian use.

Blackout orders were enforced on this once sparkling gem of an island off the Southern California coast. The Casino building was no longer lit up at night. Homes and businesses were instructed to use dark shades and curtains over their windows. Residents were forbidden to peer out of windows at night to prevent any escape of light that could allow enemies to pinpoint geographical locations.

Training to fire 22 mm guns by U.S. Navy instructors at Casino Point.

The United States Maritime Service had the largest presence on the Island at this time, occupying several Avalon hotels and other facilities and converting the Chicago Cubs spring baseball field, the hills surrounding town, and the sea itself into training areas. Over a period of 34 months from 1942 to 1945, the USMS trained tens of thousands of men for duty on "Liberty Ships," the military's supply pipeline. The Coast Guard operated a smaller training center at Two Harbors, commonly known at that time as "The Isthmus."

U.S. Army Infantry, anti-aircraft and artillery personnel stationed on Santa Catalina Island standing in front of barracks at Camp Cactus.

The U.S. Army marching on Crescent Avenue, Avalon, on Memorial Day 1942.

The only island base not used as a training center was Camp Cactus, tucked into a small valley in the mountains near Mount Orizaba. Activities there included communications, artillery gun emplacements, and the operation of radar detection systems, then a new, hush-hush technology. Army Signal Corps personnel also served there.

The smallest of the training facilities at Catalina was run by the Office of Strategic Services, the forerunner of the Central Intelligence Agency. This tiny base, top secret at the time, was located at Toyon Bay, about three miles up the coast from Avalon. This base trained men not by the thousands or the hundreds, but by the dozen.

At the close of World War II, Philip Wrigley and the Santa Catalina Island Company worked hard to bring back some semblance of normal life to the Avalon community. The Casino was once again lit up at night – a sign to all that good times had returned to the magic isle. The steamers and the *Blanche W.* returned to plying passengers cross channel and showing the world the wonders Santa Catalina Island had to offer. Many former residents and their families returned to the island they loved now that happy days were here again.

Philip Wrigley with his daughters Deedie and Blanny at El Rancho Escondido.

Arthur Meyerhoff believed Philip Wrigley's most marked personal traits were candor and fairness. A wonderful example of Philip's candor appears in his book. In 1925, when Philip was elected by the board of directors as president of William Wrigley Jr., Co., he was quoted in the *Chicago Sun-Times* (February 11, 1925) as saying, "I am by no means sure that I am succeeding on my own merits. I greatly fear … the fact that I am my father's son had much to do with my election…" Philip Knight Wrigley was nothing if not down to earth and completely straightforward.

As to his fairness, Meyerhoff noted that, though Mr. Wrigley came from a famous, wealthy family background and was highly talented and accomplished, "…in all the years I was associated with him, I never knew him to use his power to demean one in a position lower than his."

Meyerhoff writes that William Wrigley Jr.'s intention was to preserve Santa Catalina as a reminder to future generations of early California's lifestyle and charm – "a refuge…for the rich and poor." His son, Philip believed in the soundness of this approach.

Philip K. Wrigley accomplished much in a variety of fields. Many of his endeavors grew out of his family business, but aviation did not. Meyerhoff suggests "it was almost as if he were trying – solely for his own satisfaction – to succeed at something that wasn't 'passed down' from his father." From his teens onward, Philip was always tinkering with airplane engines, automobile engines, any engine.

Philip had two Dusenburgs on the island, garaged at his Avalon home, Casa del Monte on Sunshine Terrace. A Dusenburg aficionado noticed in a 1930s picture of one of these cars at El Rancho Escondido, that the bumper was upside down. Daughter Blanny says that made sense to her, because "Dad took everything apart to see how it worked and then put it back together again." Philip probably liked the look of the bumper better upside down.

In 1946, Philip Wrigley circulated a memo titled "Basic Policies." Alison Wrigley-Rusack included it in her 1994 article on her grandfather. Among the highlights:

- Turn a liability into an asset.

- Do a thorough job or don't do it at all.

- Never try to get something for nothing – it will always be worth nothing.

- Be fair and above board, not trying to gain an advantage at the expense of someone else.

Philip had many traits his employees appreciated. Showing genuine respect for staff was a characteristic he shared with his father. Meyerhoff recorded his simple explanation for this: "My father started to work when he was nine, and he never forgot what it was like to labor. Consequently, he was very considerate of his employees."

Another Meyerhoff anecdote illuminates Mr. Wrigley's integrity and innate sense of fairness.

Around 1950, a rumor circulated in Avalon that Santa Catalina Island Co. would be selling a house to "Negroes." A small but vocal delegation visited the company offices to complain. Malcolm Renton, a Santa Catalina Island Company vice president who resided in Avalon, needed to talk with Philip Wrigley about other issues as well, so he phoned him in Chicago. He explained the incident regarding the residential property sale and asked how he should handle it.

Without a moment's hesitation, Philip replied that those who were unhappy with the prospect of the sale should "read the Constitution of the United States." It would be more than a decade until equal housing legislation was enacted in America, but Philip Wrigley already knew what was right.

Helen and Philip Wrigley.

Philip realized his own hard-working father had trouble adjusting to the idea of retirement when he turned 65 in the mid-1920s. He had no hobbies or outside interests, business was his life. In fact, since he was the founder and head of the entire company, he did what he wanted to do – keep on working. "Nothing is so much fun as business," he told *Fortune* magazine. "I do not expect to do anything but work as long as I can stand up."

Philip Wrigley learned from his father's continuing zest for work past age 70. While most companies simply ushered employees out the door at 65, the Wrigley Co. under Philip originated a plan known unofficially as "on-the-job retirement training."

At 65, an employee could choose retirement with a full pension, but they also had another option. With the permission of the Retirement Committee, employees could work past 65, but had to take one month off at their own expense the first year, two months the second year, and so on. In the third year of the plan, employees would be working for the sheer enjoyment of it, since they would be creating no extra income over their pension amount.

Catalina Island Conservancy Headquarters in Avalon.

Philip Wrigley carried on and expanded his father's vision of a resort for people of moderate means and enhanced the concept of an "island in time" where the heritage of California could be preserved. Though, like his father, he had far-flung business responsibilities, he spent as much time at Catalina as possible. His experiences on the island spanned a much longer period than his father's. Philip continued to visit Catalina into his eighties, a span of nearly sixty years.

Through all of those decades, Philip was giving careful thought to Catalina's future. He was the impetus behind the creation of the Santa Catalina Island Conservancy in 1972. The Conservancy is still moving forward in its quest to protect Catalina's natural and cultural treasures, and the Wrigley family continues to be a supportive force in the organization.

Philip believed conservation and development could go hand in hand if carefully managed. He was always concerned with the immediate problems of fostering and preserving the island's plants, trees, animals, and all aspects of its natural beauty. He was considered an environmentalist long before the term was commonly used.

On April 12, 1977, Philip Knight Wrigley fell ill at his home in Lake Geneva, Wisconsin, and passed away a few hours later at a nearby hospital. He left his wife of nearly sixty years, Helen; a son, William; and two daughters, Ada Blanche and Dorothy. At distant Santa Catalina Island, where he had continued to vacation for many years, flags were flown at half-staff.

He will always be remembered for the way he lived his life, the way he treated all with whom he came in contact, and the way he loved the Island.

Looking down upon the 500 acre ranch of El Rancho Escondido.

El Rancho Escondido tour and horse show.

⌒ EL RANCHO ESCONDIDO ⌒

In 1930, Philip and Helen established a horse breeding ranch twelve miles from Avalon, atop a ridge in the rugged interior of Catalina, that raised and trained purebreds, including Arabians. This 500-acre ranch, high above Little Harbor on the island's western shore was named El Rancho Escondido – the Hidden Ranch. On working vacations, Philip and Helen would spend up to three months on Catalina each winter and spring, usually from February to May, much of the time at their ranch home.

Helen and her sister, Olive Atwater Getz, at the Ranch

Left to right on horseback, Bill, Helen, Philip, and Deedie."

The Ranch was a place where the Wrigleys were able to combine business with their love for horses and ranch life. Their children, Blanche (Blanny), Dorothy (Deedie), and Bill, all worked and played hard on these extended vacations. In recent conversations filled with reminiscences, Blanny recalled many of these experiences.

She remembered that finding the right interior island location for El Rancho Escondido was an adventure in itself. Philip, Helen, Blanny and Deedie camped out at several spots to figure out which site was best for their island retreat. This was prior to having the luxury of a tent on the island so everyone bedded down with blankets on the ground around the campfire. The family first camped in Sweet Water Canyon. Philip

determined that the chilly bottom of a canyon was not ideal, noting that the goats always bedded down in the higher hills. After the third night out, the current site of El Rancho Escondido was chosen. Blanny and her sister watched the ranch being built and even helped their father lay bricks for the companionways along the stalls.

Philip cared for Blanny and Deedie by himself during one of their visits. His culinary exploits would by no means be considered gourmet. They ended up eating a lot of baloney – fried baloney and eggs for breakfast; cold baloney sandwiches for lunch; hot baloney with macaroni and cheese for dinner.

In the background is the current ranch house. The ox cart in the foreground was imported by Philip from Mexico.

Exterior view of the ranch house. This photo was taken July 20, 1955.

El Rancho Escondido began the legacy of the Catalina Arabian breeding program. What began as an effort to improve the wild horse population on the island soon became a breeding program dedicated to pure Arabians. Under the management of people like Millard Johnson and Joe Dawkins, Catalina Arabians won many championships at horse shows across the country.

Although El Rancho Escondido's operations have changed over the years, Philip and Helen Wrigley's desire to share its beauty is being fulfilled by the Santa Catalina Island Company. The ranch is a featured stop on its Inland Motor Tour enjoyed by thousands each year. Tour guests are treated to a view of the Catalina Arabians during their visit.

Rigging the ox cart on the ranch. Left to right: Philip Wrigley; ranch manager Jack White; ranch hand Joe Machado; and unidentified ranch hand; and Dorothy A. Haw, Philip's secretary.

Philip Wrigley, with his horse Spearmint, calling his office from the only phone on the ranch.

Left to right – Hugh Smith, Sr., Blanny, unknown, Deedie, pilot Justin Dart and Walter Seiler in white cap. At the plane, Bill, Helen, unknown and Philip.

The first and only landing of an aircraft at Rancho Escondido in 1935. The plane was piloted by Justin Dart.

Today, Wrigley family members carry on the management of the Ranch, fulfilling the legacy of sharing the beauty and excitement that is El Rancho Escondido.

Las Casitas project under construction.

Las Casitas project with final stages of landscaping and walkways.

⌒ Hotels, Housing and Residential ⌒

Under Philip K. Wrigley's leadership, the island's housing needs for residents and visitors continued to grow. His tenure was a time of expansion and renovation for Catalina's hotels, multi-unit housing and residential neighborhoods.

During the 1930s, the Resorts Division of the Santa Catalina Island Company oversaw the administration of the hotels and villas offering overnight accommodations for visitors. After Pearl Harbor, the island was so deserted that the SCI Company began looking for ways to utilize their properties to assist the war effort, sending pictorial booklets of properties available for training purposes to various branches of the military.

The completed Las Casitas project.

Hotel St. Catherine beach scene.

After 1928.

The Hotel St. Catherine lobby.

The Marine Dining Room in 1938.

Hotel St. Catherine.

The Hotel Atwater, Hotel St. Catherine and Island Villas were used by the Maritime Service to house crews training at the Country Club, the Cubs ballpark and the Casino. The Las Casitas Bungalows were used as officer housing. Military families rented every available room in town to be close to their loved ones. The hotel properties suffered a tremendous amount of wear and tear during the war years, but under the leadership of Philip Wrigley and administrator Malcolm Renton, the Santa Catalina Island Company was able to renovate and repair them in time to welcome a returning tourist trade for the 1946 season. As part of that effort, individual bathrooms were added to the Hotel Atwater, which had operated with only 12 private baths and joint use facilities in the hallways since its opening in 1920.

REMOVAL OF BACK KITCHEN AND
CONVERSION TO APARTMENTS. OLD
SWIMMING POOL IN FOREGROUND 1947

The Hotel St. Catherine's back kitchen was removed for conversion of the hotel to apartments in 1947. The old swimming pool is in the foreground.

REAR OF HOTEL AFTER KITCHEN
DEMOLITION AND CONVERSION TO
APARTMENTS 1947

Rear kitchen removed and converted to apartments, 1947.

Only the Hotel St. Catherine, which suffered badly from use as a barracks, was not reopened to tourist trade. After determining that the cost of returning it to its first-class hotel status was too excessive, it was decided to turn it into apartments for employees. This usage continued until 1952, when Joe and Rose Arno began to operate the property as a suite hotel for visitors. In 1966, the Hotel St. Catherine met her demise, but memories of this beautiful hotel resort linger on in the memories of Islanders and visitors alike.

In the mid-1950s, new hotel accommodations were needed for the growing tourist trade in Avalon. In 1957, the Pavilion Lodge was built to provide deluxe but affordable housing to island visitors. Its construction coincided with the decision to demolish the 10' x 12' cottages of the Island Villas, which were not much better than tents and did not compare with present-day motels.

DEMOLITION OF HOTEL 1966

Final demolition of the Hotel St. Catherine/Apartments in 1966.

Hamilton Cove construction.

On the right is Mr. James E. Townsend, Vice President of SCI Co., witnessing the Hamilton Cove Balboa Bay Club Lease with the president of the Balboa Bay Club. 1964-1974.

During the 1970s, Avalon experienced an unusual housing boom. Three new developments were initiated: the 72-unit Sol Vista, the 48-unit Fairview Terrace and the Canyon Terrace apartment projects by Al Solomon, A 330-unit Hamilton Beach project by the Balboa Bay Club, now known as Hamilton Cove Resorts was constructed during the 1980s. These housing developments marked the first introduction of condominium development in Avalon and the first construction of speculative, for-sale housing for residents and visitors in more than 30 years. Although condominium ownership was popular throughout Southern California, Avalon was an untried market, and condo development, especially on leased land, was not particularly well known.

The Hamilton Cove project represented Catalina's learning curve in dealing with large-scale, highly complex condo development in a new era of increasing government and environmental regulation. This project thoroughly tested the combined skills and patience of SCI Company and the City of Avalon in administering a development of this magnitude.

The dramatic concept of a secluded, high quality residential resort complex perched on the hillsides of Hamilton Cove originally appeared in the SCI Company 1962 Master Plan and was later ratified in the 1968 City of Avalon Master Plan. Aside from being a highly challenging site, the Hamilton Cove project heralded many "firsts:"

• The first City of Avalon Development Agreement.

• The first application of the City Housing Ordinance, requiring builders of resort condominiums to provide affordable housing equal to 25% of the estimated number of units in the development (resulting in what is now "New Tremont Street Housing").

• The first annexation of land into the City of Avalon since its incorporation in 1913.

• The first Avalon project subject to the rules of the newly formed California Coastal Commission, which required the developer to augment the City of Avalon water supply and construct a 200-person campground.

Hamilton Cove construction.

Hamilton Cove construction.

The requirements of the Coastal Commission led to the creation of the R.O. Desalination Plant at Pebbly Beach Edison plant and Hermit Gulch Campground in Avalon Canyon. To accommodate the affordable housing obligation, SCI Company relocated the development's bus maintenance garage, vehicle fuel station and laundry from lower Tremont Street to Pebbly Beach, providing a site for the required 68 units of housing.

Almost 15 years after commencement of grading, the first phase of 165 units at Hamilton Cove was completed and sold in the early 1990s. The project received several awards from the architectural and building industry for design excellence and construction ingenuity. The reverse osmosis seawater desalination plant created to augment the Avalon water supply was highly publicized. Of special significance to drought-plagued water authorities throughout the State, it was the first seawater desalination plant in California constructed to augment a community potable water supply. The plant is now owned and operated by Southern California Edison.

Beacon Street Apartments, 1967, by Al Solomon.

Another affordable multiple unit housing development was created at Beacon and Clemente Streets by Al Solomon in association with SCI Company as a co-venture with architect William Pereira, planner of the Santa Catalina Island Master Plan and General Plan for the City of Avalon. This was Al's first residential construction project in Avalon and although it was a small, 15-unit structure, it fell hostage to its share of "Catalina Factor" cost and timing overruns. Al handled these issues, and the project ultimately succeeded.

The 72-unit Sol Vista condo project was intended to provide housing opportunities for both Avalon residents and vacation homebuyers. Completed in 1974, they were fully sold in a very short period of time. So ended the first test of the condo market in Avalon. About ten years later, approximately 50% of the units were occupied by full-time Avalon residents who either owned or rented their units.

Private home being constructed on middle Terrace road in Avalon.

Groundbreaking on Wrigley Terrace road Apartments built by the Smyth Brothers Construction Company. Left to right-unknown, Mayor Herbert Wegmann, unknown, Charles Smyth, Edward Smyth, unknown, Malcolm Renton, President, SCICo., 1966.

Fairview construction.

Fairview construction.

Tremont Street with Eucalyptus Hill in foreground.

The site of 80 new homes to be built on Eucalyptus Hill, between the Tremont Street apartments and the Catalina Canyon Hotel.

❧ VISITOR SERVICES ❧

The Santa Catalina Island Company opened the island's first Visitor Information and Services Center in 1971 in the former baggage room of the steamer terminal. The design concept and operational program for the Center were laid out and monitored by Philip and Helen Wrigley. The purpose of the Center was to sell more SCICo tours and hotel accommodations and provide visitors with general educational information on the Island.

Philip Wrigley had a special interest in vehicles, transportation and all things mechanical, so when a need surfaced in the early 1970s to replace the obsolete 1930 vintage touring buses with larger tractor-trailer and tandem mini-buses, the project commanded his personal detailed attention.

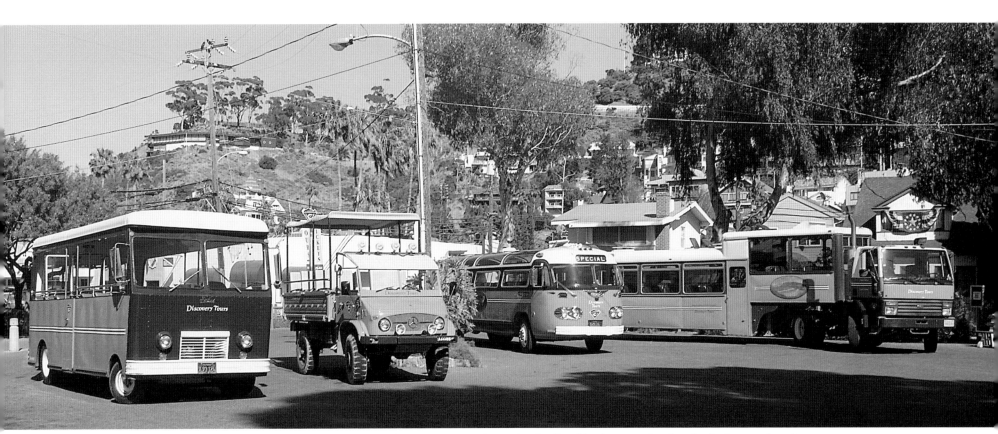

The Island Plaza 2005 offers park like public setting, and serves as the Transportation Center for Catalina Island tours and a place for food rest and service.

Left to right, Malcolm J. Renton, Senior Vice President and Director of Santa Catalina Island Company 1929-1975; Philip K. Wrigley, Vice President 1920-1925, President 1925-1962, and Chairman of the WM. Wrigley Jr. Company; Ernest Debbs, Los Angeles County Supervisor.

PERSONAL REMEMBRANCES ABOUT PHILIP K. WRIGLEY

These excerpts of personal remembrances are reproduced from the Santa Catalina Island Company's 1994 special edition Water Lines newsletter.

DOUG BOMBARD: President of Doug Bombard Enterprises and Catalina Channel Express.

My overall remembrances of Philip Wrigley are that he was the first environmentalist I knew, which was long before the word was commonly used. He was very concerned that any development on Catalina Island be done properly.

I was making a proposal to lengthen the sewer outfall at Isthmus Cove, and Mr. Wrigley shocked me with the statement he did not feel we should be discharging our sewer into the ocean. I found him very knowledgeable regarding sewer treatment plants which I didn't know existed at that time, and which he instructed us to look into. As a result of his foresight and direction, we installed our first sewer treatment plant at the Isthmus in the 60's.

SHIRLEY DAVY: Avalon City Clerk from 1964-to present and mainstay of BBDO during its entire 37 year presence in Avalon, stepping down from that capacity as Vice President of BBDO Chicago when the Avalon offices closed in 1993.)

One day, during one of Mr. Wrigley's spring visits to Catalina Island, Bob Gingrich from the Chicago BBDO office and I went to see him to discuss something that only required two minutes of time. As we were leaving, Mr. Wrigley asked us to come back in and close the door. Bob and I were a little anxious about this unexpected private meeting as we returned to our seats.

The meeting ended about two hours later and we left having thoroughly enjoyed two hours of Mr. Wrigley's reminiscences about boat engines, funny things that had happened to him and the "good old day." It was a delightful afternoon.

HARVEY COWELL: Drove buses for SCI Company from 1935 until WWII and after the War, worked for Wilmington Transportation Company for a couple of years. He served on the Avalon City council for 20 years, serving as Mayor from 1952-1956 and 1969-1972.

My introduction to Mr. Wrigley was at a meeting in which he announced that the Catalina Steamship Line would be taking the steamer *SS Catalina* off the run during the winter months.

Recalling this encounter and reflecting on the development of cross channel transportation has helped me understand what Mr. Wrigley had in mind and why he took this action. He not only needed to slow the losses during the winter months, but conduct a long range search for boats that would better serve our community and also give others who might be interested in providing cross channel transportation an opportunity to become involved.

The *SS Catalina* used to leave Wilmington in the morning, arrive in Avalon at approximately 11:00 a.m. and then depart the Island at 3:45 p.m., taking most of Avalon's visitors with it. At one of our meetings, Mr. Wrigley said that he did not feel Avalon could survive on a "one steamer-a-day" economy. He suggested what was needed was transportation the likes of which had been serving New York City and Long Island, small, fast boats and frequent scheduling.

During the first years without the big white steamer, a number of boat owners expressed an interest in entering Catalina's transportation. For the most part, however, they were not interested during the winter months as long as the steamer was in the picture. None were interested in investing funds in the development of modern equipment until Catalina Cruises built its fleet. The rest is history and I believe Mr. Wrigley deserves much credit for the laying of the groundwork for today's modern cross channel transportation.

I am reminded of an incident when a local lady who had just purchased a home just below his in Avalon. She sought out Mr. Wrigley in the company office to complain about the trees on his property that were shedding leaves and filling the roof gutters at her home.

She wanted to see Mr. Wrigley personally, and in her visit to the company office she ran into a man in a jumpsuit who stopped and asked if he could help her. She replied that she was looking for Mr. Wrigley. He replied "I am Mr. Wrigley." She discussed the problem with him and was assured it would be remedied.

In parting, she thanked him and apologized for taking his time. His reply was, "I am never too busy to visit with my neighbors."

JACK FENNIE: Owner and operator of Catalina Island Freight Lines from 1964 to 2005. Jack worked for the Santa Catalina Island Company for 17 years in various management capacities including Vice President and Treasurer.

Mr. Wrigley usually put in a full day of work at the office. He was in the office during the normal workday hours, lunched with business associates, and finished the day at home by working alone at night.

I learned almost too late to do me much good that the best time to approach him with a problem was by phone late at night. Never did he sound annoyed: more likely, he appeared grateful for the call and, with his undivided time and attention more could be accomplished. He seemed to enjoy work more than leisure; even more than sleep.

My observation is that prominent families often have prominent children, outstandingly bad. Even ordinary families often have rotten kids. Not Mr. Wrigley though! I can't imagine anyone having a better family. They were all distinctively individual, all simply great and fun to be with.

One plan of Mr. Wrigley's was well known. He was immensely proud of his son who he hoped would eventually succeed him. He did succeed him and, apparently, with great success. One who perhaps knew this better than anyone was Mr. Wrigley's nephew, Bud Offield. Our paths crossed frequently in those later years. Although Mr. Offield was retired and professed to have nothing to do with the business, he was full of stories about its growth and prosperity and proud of the work of his cousin.

This brings up an important point. During all of those years, and with all the family members involved, I have never heard one unkind word by one about another. They will probably pull together forever.

Regardless of all this, the continued success of the Wrigley Family has to be a miracle.

BLANNY AVALON HAGENAH: Daughter of Philip and Helen Wrigley's older daughter, Ada Blanche. Blanny and her brothers and cousins joined the Wrigleys for holiday and family get-togethers at the Arizona Biltmore and at Catalina and spent childhood summers with the Wrigleys at their home in Lake Geneva, Wisconsin.

Almost a dozen grandchildren have fond and very vivid memories of a wonderful man. To many others Philip K. Wrigley was a businessman, an aviator, a baseball team owner, a mechanic; to us he was our grandfather and we call him "Daddy Phil."

Daddy Phil inspired in us a "can do" attitude, not by words, but by actions. He encouraged us to pursue many skills and interests and often included us as he demonstrated his: working a drill, sailing an iceboat, welding an axle, tuning an engine, riding a horse, racing a speedboat, driving a jeep, shooting a revolver, piloting a plane. His motto was "If a job's worth doing, then it's worth doing right."

Daddy Phil always took an interest in the many and varied facets of his grandchildren's lives. During my college and early career years he wrote to me often and encouraged me in my goals. We shared a love of Catalina, and he happily corresponded with me about his plans for the Conservancy, his father's "foresightedness" and his own "hard work to preserve in its natural state at least a little chunk of Southern California." Daddy Phil loved the island very much.

I remember my grandfather with great affection and respect. He demonstrated humility, decency, and integrity. It was a joy and a privilege to know Philip K. Wrigley, the man we called "Daddy Phil."

RUDY PILTCH: Former Senior Vice President and Director of Planning for Santa Catalina Island Company; also former Mayor of Avalon.

In 1970, SCI Company initiated a redecorating program for the interior of the Las Casitas units, which Mr. & Mrs. Wrigley took great interest in reviewing when they were in Avalon. During one of their inspection tours, Mr. Wrigley noted that many of the windows were mechanically activated by a small, rather intricate, metal crank handle that opened and closed the window from the inside; however, most of the crank handles were missing. I reported to Mr. Wrigley that due to the vintage of the windows our purchasing agent was having difficulty finding a supplier for the crank handles. Upon the completion of our inspection tour Mr. Wrigley asked if he could take one of the handles back to Chicago. Two weeks later we received a heavy package with about a dozen window crank handles identical to the one we had given Mr. Wrigley. When I asked who the supplier was, Mr. Wrigley informed me that he was! He had made each one in his home shop at Lake Geneva and he said, "If you need any more just let me know!"

A. DOUGLAS PROPST: Spent 40 years on Catalina Island – the first 20 of which were with the Santa Catalina Island Company in charge of the range management program and the last two decades of which were with the Conservancy. In 1993 he retired as the Conservancy President.

Philip Wrigley was a hands-on person, that is he liked to do things with his own hands particularly mechanical things. He very much appreciated good tools and machinery and enjoyed seeing same maintained and used properly. But, if something should happen to break, as it did on one of the property tours, he would fix it right there if possible. I remember a bump gate incident at Middle Ranch, when the gate did not function properly. He was out of the car in a flash with a handful of good tools, the gate was soon repaired and we were on our way.

He enjoyed innovative ideas; for instance, something you might have devised to provide an easier, more efficient way of getting a particular job done. On one of his visits to Middle Ranch, I told Mr. Wrigley that we had a very good crop of oats and asked if he would like to go up to the field for a firsthand look. He said, "Oh I'll take your word for that, what have you fellows built in the shop that I would like to see?"

As good luck would have it, we had just built, tested, and put finishing touches on a power driven wire roller that we were using to roll up the many miles of old barbed wire and phone lines that were laying around Catalina. This contraption involved the use of a Briggs-Stratton engine, an old truck differential, and some old disk blades made into the spools. For mobility the whole works was mounted on the front of an old GI four-by-four and one man could run it. It wasn't beautiful, but it worked, and Mr. Wrigley loved it.

Again, he appreciated good equipment and was much more apt to approve the purchase of a top of the line machine rather than the economy model. He always said, "You get what you pay for."

MALCOLM J. RENTON: Mr. Renton retired from the Santa Catalina Island Company in 1975 after 43 years of service. During that time he worked for Mr. Wrigley in various capacities such as assistant, corporate secretary, and Vice President.

There were many exciting and memorable experiences that I had the privilege of enjoying while growing up in Catalina as an eleven-year-old boy, and later working for Mr. Philip K. Wrigley, after the death of his father, Mr. Wm. Wrigley Jr. in 1932. It is difficult for me to select just a few to relate, because Mr. Wrigley was more to me than my boss – he and his lovely wife Helen were very good friends.

I like to think back when I was growing up, of the wonderful relationship my father, D.M. Renton, had with the Wrigley family. It was during this time that Mr. Philip Wrigley would do special things for me such as sending me through the Wm. Wrigley Jr. chewing gum factory and many more treats for a small boy growing up. And later, when I did join the Santa Catalina Island Company as Mr. Philip Wrigley's assistant, I became closer to his way of doing things and enjoyed the friendship of his entire family.

The planning and construction of the Hamilton Beach amphibian airport was another project that Mr. Wrigley assigned to me. He had me draw up the plans for the terminal building and supervise the entire development, under the watchful eye of my father. He wanted a Spanish style structure with a tower and a patio for viewing the airplane operations. The ground floor lobby was to be devoted to the passengers, having open arches at two sides, overlooking attractive gardens and the amphibian ramp from the ocean.

The lobby had a ticket office, a refreshment counter, and restroom facilities. Catalina Tile was used on the floor, walls, and roof. The second floor was occupied by the offices of the "Wilmington-Catalina Airlines" which incidentally was started as an independent company by Mr. Wrigley to promote air travel to Catalina.

One particular feature of the airport was the installation of the turntable at the top of the ramp. This allowed the amphibian planes to be turned around ready to descend the ramp again into the ocean for take off. The turntable was Mr. Wrigley's idea for handling the planes in a very narrow area surrounded by mountains.

Many more interesting projects together with meeting famous personages and friends of Mr. and Mrs. Philip Wrigley made my relationship with my boss a most enjoyable one. I admired him and enjoyed working for him and the Santa Catalina Island Company.

Catalina Airport at Hamilton Beach.

HUGH T. "BUD" SMITH: Retired United Airlines pilot, an Avalon native and former Avalon City Councilman and Mayor of the City of Avalon.

As long as I can remember, my parents always spoke of Mr. Philip Wrigley with high regard and admiration. All through my childhood my father worked for Mr. Wrigley and the Santa Catalina Island Company. In 1939, Mr. Wrigley loaned my father the money and equipment to become an independent contractor in the road construction and dirt moving business, with an agreement that he would be able to bid on all Island Company work as well as any other outside jobs.

In about 1937 Mr. Wrigley asked my Dad to grade the road and clear the brush on the ridge directly to the west of Rancho Escondido. It is a very gradual sloping ridge and quite wide. Some 4000 feet of area was to be cleared. Mr. Wrigley was very interested in aviation. He had a good friend, a Mr. Justin Dart, who wanted Mr. Wrigley to buy an airplane to commute from Chicago to Catalina Island and to land just minutes away from his El Rancho Escondido. The aircraft was a twin engine Lockheed Vega. At the planned time, Mr. Dart roared overhead, checked the roughly prepared road, looked at the smoke coming from the smudge pots, which were placed near the road to obtain an idea of the prevailing wind, and proceeded to make a perfect landing. Mr. Wrigley and all of his family were there on horseback to greet the airplane. All of the SCI Company brass, as well as my Dad and I, were there too.

What a thrill it was for this young boy who was already interested in becoming a pilot! Mr. Wrigley, observing my excitement, asked me to go aboard the airplane with him. That I will never forget. Over the years I reminded him, and thanked him several times for that thoughtful deed to this young wide-eyed boy.

DR. NORMAN TOPPING: Late Chancellor Emeritus of the University of Southern California and former SCI Company Board Member – extracted from his book "Recollections," co-authored by Gordon Cohn.

In 1962, the Santa Catalina Island Company which was owned by P.K. Wrigley had Bill Pereira do a study of Catalina Island and make recommendations for its future.

My wife Helen and I flew back with the Pereiras, who had invited us to have dinner with Mr. and Mrs. Wrigley in Chicago. Bill presented P.K. with the results of his study on the island. One of the major recommendations was that a marine science center should be developed. Mr. and Mrs. Wrigley were very interested. Later studies ended up recommending Big Fisherman's Cove for the site. Mr. Wrigley agreed to deed to the University the necessary land and to set up a buffer zone so that there could not be development around the site. We soon secured a $500,000 grant and added it to some private contributions and University funds and built the laboratories at Fisherman's Cove.

During those years (when) the Wrigleys visited the island they usually would drive up to the Isthmus and we would meet them and show them the laboratories. Mr. Wrigley was particularly interested in the hyperbaric chamber. On one of those trips I talked to him about the possibilities of more land. Shortly thereafter I received a communication from Mr. Wrigley saying there might be a better way than a gift of land. That idea became a gift of some shares of the Santa Catalina Island Company by Mr. Wrigley and his sister, Mrs. Offield, to USC.

The University's entire relationship with the Wrigleys developed because we had dinner that night in Chicago. After that meeting, whenever I was in Chicago, I would drop in to see Mr. Philip Wrigley and he would take me to lunch in the Wrigley Building. In 1978, William Wrigley, P.K.'s only son, asked me to join the Board of the Santa Catalina Island Company. Bill Wrigley (became) a trustee of the University of Southern California. We are very closely associated.

William "Bill" Wrigley
Born 1933 – Died 1999
The Legacy Continues

ISLAND ACHIEVEMENTS - 1961 to 1999

Environmental Education & Conservation
Open Space Easement Signed with Los Angeles County
Land Use Plan Changed & Certified
    (88% of island shifted from ranch to ecological preserve)
Local Coastal Plan for Santa Catalina Island Approved & Certified
Donor Trustee of University of Southern California for
    Wrigley Institute of Environmental Studies at Two Harbors
Named Philip K. Wrigley Marine Science Center

Opened Land for Public & Private Building Projects
Expansion of Avalon Public Schools
Affordable Housing in Avalon –
    Beacon Hill, Bird Park, Eucalyptus Hill, Fairview, Sol Vista
SCI Co. and City of Avalon Develop City Hall,
    Recreation, and Fire Station

Tourism & Entertainment
SCI Co. Assumes Operation of Casino Ballroom, Avalon Theatre (both
    refurbished & renovated), Descanso Beach
Steamer Terminal Building Rebuilt & Reopened as Restaurants,
    Retail Shops
SCI Co. Reassumes Operation of Pavilion Lodge & Hotel Atwater
Island Plaza Sightseeing Area Upgraded
Opening of Visitors Information Center in Avalon
Wrigley Memorial & Botanical Garden Merged With Catalina
    Island Conservancy
Tour Bus Garage & Service Station Relocated to Pebbly Beach

Public Utilities & Services
SCI Co. & Southern California Edison Seawater Desalination
    Viability Study
15-Year Concept Plan Environmental Impact Report Certified
Pebbly Beach Freight & Commercial Area Improvements
Cabrillo Mole Shore Area & Avalon Cemetery Deeded to City of Avalon
Casino Fuel Dock Sold to City of Avalon

Decentralization From Chicago Corporate Office
Election of Paxson H. Offield to President of SCI Co.

Deedie and Bill Wrigley

PART THREE
WILLIAM WRIGLEY
THE LEGACY CONTINUES

PRESIDENT OF WM. WRIGLEY JR. CO.
1961 TO *1999*

William "Bill" Wrigley was born to Helen Atwater and Philip Knight Wrigley on January 21, 1933 and grew up in Chicago, Illinois. He always looked forward to the long annual visits to Santa Catalina with his family. The keen enthusiasms of his youth included a fondness for animals, especially horses and dogs, performing magic shows for family and friends, and, not surprisingly, Chicago Cubs baseball. Happily for young Bill, the springtime visits to Avalon partly overlapped with the Cubs spring training camp there during the 1930s and 1940s.

Young "Billy" was a Cubs Fan from the beginning.

Young Bill Wrigley practicing with his lasso on the lawn at El Rancho Escondido.

Bill's sister Blanny recalls many happy times with her brother on the Island when they were children. One of her earliest memories is from El Rancho Escondido. Blanny and sister, Deedie, had white mice as pets at the ranch. The mice got loose, bred with the wild mice on the property, and soon the ranch house was full of mice. "Billy" was approximately three months old at the time, and mother Helen was afraid of the mice getting to her baby son. She told Philip to do something about it, and he did. He took pie pans and cut holes in them, then slipped the legs of the crib into the holes, making it almost impossible for a mouse to climb into the crib with baby Bill. This seemed to satisfy Helen until they could find a way to eradicate the mice altogether.

Helen Wrigley holding two grandsons, Will and Phil Hagenah, with son Bill at right.

Like his older sisters, Bill was taught the value of money early and was encouraged to save. As a child, he kept the money he earned from chores in a set of nested apples – much like the popular Russian nested dolls. One way he earned his money was by running errands for his sisters, Blanny and Deedie. The girls paid him one penny for every ten errands that he did.

One day, Bill asked the girls to take him to a store so he could buy a present for his mother. He selected a pretty brooch and then proceeded to carefully open one apple after another until he got to the smallest apple at the center for his change. The poor store clerk was getting rather impatient with the whole process. When Bill finally removed all his money, he was short one penny. Sister Blanny came up with the extra coin on the condition that Bill would do another ten errands for her in payment of his debt.

Members of the Wrigley family have often been observed paying their own way to events or at venues that are a part of the Wrigley Company sphere of influence, demonstrating core values that have been passed down from generation to generation.

Bill Wrigley attended preparatory school at Deerfield Academy in Massachusetts, then Yale University, where he graduated with a degree in psychology in 1954. He was the first in the Wrigley legacy line to graduate from college, and the modern business processes he learned at Yale shaped the future growth of the entire Wrigley Company enterprise.

The quiet, somewhat shy boy had grown into a quiet and polite man. His friends and business associates knew him as a kind, considerate companion, endowed with a wonderful sense of humor.

Blanny, Bill, and Deedie at El Rancho Escondido, 1977.

Bill Wrigley, sister Blanny, son Bill Jr., and John Hagenah on a boat excursion, 1998.

Bill Wrigley served two years of active duty with the United States Navy in the Pacific and over twenty years in the Naval Reserve. He retired from the Reserve in 1977 with the rank of Lieutenant Commander. Like his father, Bill was proud of the time that he spent in military service to his country.

Bill was married to the former Alison Hunter from 1957 until their divorce. They have three children, Alison, Philip, and William, Jr. In 1981, Bill married Julie Burns, an environmentalist and attorney.

Through the years, Bill Wrigley was a trim and vigorous man, always finding enjoyment in outdoor recreation. In his sixties, he wore his silver hair in an ivy-league style befitting his Yale background.

His professional career was full and varied. He was President and Chief Executive Officer of Wm Wrigley Jr. Company, the world's largest manufacturer of chewing gum, for 38 years. During his tenure, he established a strategic direction from which he never wavered.

"Geographic diversification" was the watchword for the Wrigley Company's management. While Bill was at the helm sales soared from $100 million to $2 billion. The number of countries with awareness of the Wrigley brand went from a few dozen to over 140. Those close to Bill recall his work ethic, and cite him as someone who always provided an excellent model of conduct for associates and friends.

Ronald C. Doutt, President and COO of the Santa Catalina Island Company, notes that Bill Wrigley brought the Wm Wrigley Jr. Company into the computer age by installing one of the very first IBM computer systems at the company's corporate office in Chicago. The massive installation took up the whole tenth floor of the Wrigley building, and the entire heating and air-conditioning system had to be revamped to accommodate this "high tech" behemoth. This upgrade, which looked toward the 21st century, spilled over to Santa Catalina Island Company corporate business operations as well.

According to Mr. Doutt: "The resiliency of the Wrigley ownership legacy has now extended well into the fourth generation. That is generally a time in the life cycle of other family businesses when dramatic refocusing of interest and efforts if not outright sale or dissolution is common. In the case of Catalina Island and the Santa Catalina Island Co., however, and despite an ownership tenure that now spans an 86-year period of wars, depression, recession, tax law changes, economic/building challenges – the commitment of the present Wrigley family ownership of SCICo to the betterment of Catalina Island is unwavering. Part of that phenomenon is a function of a deeply ingrained family love of Catalina; part is a unique appreciation of the history and special nature of this place; but most of it is a function of the family's 'schooling' of each succeeding generation in what I like to characterize as doing the right thing in the right way.

"At the time of Mr. Philip Wrigley's death, the majority of SCICo's land holdings had been transferred to the newly formed not-for-profit Catalina Island Conservancy and Wrigley family interests in SCICo were now held in various trust for the benefit of future Wrigley and Offield generations. William 'Bill' Wrigley and Wrigley 'Bud' Offield held voting control of most of these family trusts.

"Just as Philip Wrigley had become involved with Catalina at an early age and was thus prepared to assume the mantle of ownership responsibility upon his father's death in 1932, so too did Philip Wrigley involve his son, Bill, in the affairs of SCICo (and later the Conservancy as well) at an early age. At the time of Philip Wrigley's death in 1977, Bill Wrigley was in his early 40's and had already been a SCICo officer and director for 13 years. That experience plus his willingness to seek out and use the advice and counsel of many of his father's advisors made Bill Wrigley's process of assuming ownership responsibilities relatively smooth. Art Meyerhoff, Claude Brooks and Bud Maxwell were especially helpful with the transition. Although retired, Malcolm Renton was available as well.

"One of the most significant and far reaching early decisions of Bill Wrigley's was to talk his second cousin, Paxson (Packy) Offield, who is 'Bud' Offield's son and Dorothy Wrigley Offield's grandson, into leaving his teaching post at the Catalina Island School for Boys at Toyon Bay to come to work for the Santa Catalina Island Company. This happened in 1979 – the 60th year of Wrigley family ownership of SCICo. This move was fortuitous and timely for many reasons. Packy proved to be a 'quick study.'

Philip K. Wrigley Marine Science Center at Two Harbors, Santa Catalina Island.

"Bill Wrigley's commitments to his 'regular job' as President and CEO of the gum company limited his ability to devote as much time as was needed at SCICo and on Santa Catalina Island. His choice of Packy, in effect, was the start of a gradual but ultimately complete and successful, transition of authority and responsibility for Santa Catalina Island Company matters from Chicago to Avalon, and from the third generation of Wrigleys to the fourth."

Although Bill Wrigley believed in maintaining a low profile, he was very active in other business organizations. He was a long-time director of Texaco, Inc., American Home Products Corp., and of the Chicago Cubs baseball team where he served for 25 years.

His relationship with the Cubs had many facets. He was first and foremost a fan who spent many days at Wrigley Field cheering on his team. In the late 1970s, the organization required a great deal of capital from both park operations and organizational standpoints. Wrigley couldn't reasonably raise these funds, and with an estate tax obligation pending after the death of his parents, it became inevitable that the team would be sold. Bill was insistent that the potential buyers keep the team in Chicago and have "sufficient reputation and integrity to maintain the standards of professional baseball in general and continue support of the organization of baseball."

Bill was also a director of the Santa Catalina Island Company for four decades, much of this tenure as executive committee of the board. Throughout his life, Santa Catalina Island held a special place for Bill Wrigley. His deep concern for the success of the community of Avalon and the conservation of the Island's natural resources were issues to which he dedicated his life.

A press release at his death stated, "as a benefactor and life member of the Santa Catalina Island Conservancy, his constant tenacity and dedication helped to ensure that the grandeur and beauty of the Island's interior would be available for future generations of visitors to enjoy."

Tony Michaels, Director of USC's Marine Science Center at Two Harbors, explained Bill Wrigley's love of Catalina this way:

"The third in a line of Catalina patrons, William Wrigley demonstrated his loyalty to the island almost from day one of his stewardship. Forced to sell off family assets to settle the huge estate taxes after both his parents died in 1977, Wrigley chose his beloved Catalina over his also beloved Chicago Cubs. Reluctantly, Wrigley sold an 80 percent stake in the ball club for $20.5 million.

"Over the years William Wrigley continued to carry on his family's conservationist legacy and its support of USC projects on Catalina. Their passion for the natural wonder of Catalina has provided both a paradisaical wilderness sanctuary and a near-perfect

laboratory for environmental studies."

It was due to this deep concern for the environment that Bill Wrigley joined with the University of Southern California and the Santa Catalina Island Conservancy to fund the USC Wrigley Institute for Environmental Studies. He maintained close ties to USC and the Wrigley Institute as well as to the Philip K. Wrigley Marine Science Center near Two Harbors on Santa Catalina Island.

Although the legacy of conservation for Santa Catalina Island began with Bill Wrigley's grandfather, William Wrigley Jr. and continued with Bill's father, Philip, it was Bill Wrigley himself who completed the work of implementing the preservation plan for the island. Bill's grandfather communicated his desire to see the island and its natural resources protected for all people and future generations to enjoy. His father, Philip had set in motion the process that would fulfill that desire.

Photos above show classes taught at the Marine Science Center. At right, Author Bill White does research with Center staff member Ellen Kelly.

Bill Wrigley, third from right, at dedication of monument recalling the Chicago Cubs Spring Training Camp in Avalon Canyon, 1921 – 1951.

In the early 1960s, working with architect William Pereira and Associates, Philip began laying down a masterplan for Santa Catalina Island. It included forming a protective conservation organization to care for a large part of the island, maintaining it in its natural state. After much research, using recent "Open Space Easement" government legislation, they determined that a private non-profit conservancy could be formed to care for the island and its resources. Even areas initially excluded by the legislation were eventually included in the Santa Catalina Island Conservancy plan. They included some of the occupied coves on the island, such as White's Landing.

Building on Philip's initial implementation of a conservation plan for Santa Catalina Island, Bill devoted much of his life to seeing that plan completed and expanded beyond the vision of his father and grandfather. Bill forged a deep and meaningful relationship between the Wrigley family enterprises and the University of Southern California through the creation of the USC Wrigley Institute for Environmental Studies and the

Philip K. Wrigley Marine Science Center at Big Fisherman's Cove near Two Harbors. Bill and Julie were instrumental in the development of this program and its home on the island – both committed to the legacy of preservation and conservation begun by previous generations of the Wrigley family.

In the 1970s during Bill Wrigley's leadership of Santa Catalina Island, the USC Conference Center at Mt. Ada in Avalon operated for a number of years under the watchful eye and management of Cheryl Wagner, wife of Charlie Wagner, then City Manager of Avalon. Although USC owned the building, the title to the land was held by the Santa Catalina Island Conservancy. Eventually USC relinquished its operation and a long-term lease was assigned to a corporation, Mt. Ada Inn, Inc., operated today by innkeepers Marlene MacAdam and Susie Griffin. They are corporate shareowners along with other local residents of the island.

Sisters Deedie and Blanny, enjoying time with Bill Wrigley at a family celebration.

Bill Wrigley demonstrated the same dedication in his civic and charitable contributions as he did with the Wrigley Company and the Cubs. He served as a trustee of Northwestern Memorial Hospital of Chicago for more than 22 years, and was a trustee of USC from 1981 until his death in 1999.

In January of 1999, Mr. Wrigley was injured in a fall at his home in Lake Geneva, Wisconsin during an ice storm. He later contracted pneumonia and died at Northwestern Memorial Hospital in Chicago on March 8, 1999, with his family at his bedside.

On hearing of Bill's passing, Steve Sample, president of USC, said, "The environment and USC have lost a true friend ... Bill Wrigley was a model university trustee. He had a unique vision for teaching and research in ... environmental studies, and was willing to invest generously to make that vision a reality."

On March 29, 1999, a memorial service was held for Mr. Wrigley at Avalon's Casino Theatre. Rose Ellen Gardner, president and CEO of the Santa Catalina Island Conservancy, reminisced about her friend and colleague. She told the mourners that the Conservancy had lost "a friend, a supporter ... and a lover of nature; however, the examples he set for us – honesty, good business principles, kindness – remain with us forever..."

An obituary by City News Service noted while chairman of the Wm Wrigley Jr. Company, a corporation of international scope, William Wrigley remained a very accessible, down-to-earth individual. He was known to write personally to customers who had complained, and to answer his own office telephone.

Ronald Doutt also shared this story about Bill: "Mr. Wrigley was especially adamant that one should mean what one says and say what one means. Often a letter prepared for his signature would come back with revisions in his handwriting that were grammatically superior and provided a tightened more accurate message. Some time ago, I bought a share of Wm. Wrigley Jr. Co. stock as a gift for my niece when she was born. As a presumptuous, fairly new employee, but mindful that Mr. Wrigley's time was precious, I took the liberty to author a letter to my little niece welcoming her into the world and extolling the virtues of thrift and investment. I planned on having that letter accompany the stock certificate and that it be signed by Mr. Wrigley. When I approached Mr. Wrigley with the request, he read my typed "final" version of the letter (which I had put on SCICo letterhead) and, to my horror, said, "No, I won't sign it." Instead, he rewrote it completely (doing a much better job), included some nice personal sentiments and put it on his own stationery. It's framed in my niece's bedroom. With stock splits, that one share is now nearly 20."

Succeeding William "Bill" Wrigley as President of the Wrigley Company is his son, William Wrigley Jr., who continues to accelerate the worldwide growth and prosperity of the company. At a memorial service held on March 12, 1999 at the Fourth Presbyterian Church in Chicago, he presented the following eulogy for his father, which was

published in "A Remembrance" by the William Wrigley Jr. Company:

"Dad was a kind and gentle man, generous from the heart, and a man who cared for and respected people and their lives. It did not matter who they happened to be, he gave equal care and compassion to all who were fortunate enough to cross his path. He bestowed values of fairness, integrity, loyalty, and dependability. He was a man of his word and one you could count on for anything. His prescience was unmatched and, as a result, he took many steps that will have a lasting, positive impact for some time to come.

"To understand this man is to understand his quiet strength, his clarity through simplicity, and his commitment to excellence. Dad was a 110 percent participant in all that he did as shown in his focused energy, remarkable memory, and meticulous attention to detail.

"Dad loved many things in life – his family and friends; he loved nature, being outdoors, and animals of all kinds. He especially loved his dogs, being on the water in a boat, his horses, magic tricks, Lake Geneva, Santa Catalina Island, baseball and, of course, the business. There are also many fond memories of his wonderful sense of humor and the mischievous side that went with it.

"As for business, Dad was an inspiration to us all. He had a favorite quote from my great-grandfather who started the business in 1891: 'Life and business are rather simple, after all. To make a success of either, you've got to hang on to the knack of putting yourself in the other fellow's place.' Dad was an expert at this and never lost sight of that simple principle.

"While his passing was sudden and a shock to all of us, he would not have wanted it to be a belabored affair. I take comfort in knowing that this great man, who I am proud to call my father, is at peace. As he would wish, I will move on, carrying forward and cherishing the many lessons of his spirit."

Just two weeks prior to his passing, Bill Wrigley wrote to the author expressing appreciation for a copy of the first edition of our book, *Santa Catalina Island: Its Magic, People, and History* that we sent him. Near the close of the letter, he wrote, "I do not spend as much time on Catalina as I would like ... it is a very special place."

CROSS-CHANNEL TRANSPORTATION

During the 1970s, important changes in island transportation became a key factor in Avalon's changing economy. This period saw a new generation of smaller, faster cross-channel boats. Harbor Cruises, later named Catalina Cruises, introduced their new service in 1970 with frequent, reliable, comfortable and affordable year-round daily service to the Island. They started out with two steel-hulled, 149-passenger boats, the *Condor* and the *Eagle*, which made the trip in 1-3/4 hours. With the final departure of the *SS Catalina* in 1975, Catalina Cruises became the prime transportation service from both Long Beach and San Pedro to the island. In 1982, Doug Bombard and Tom Rudder introduced a new generation of comfortable high-speed, high-tech passenger boats under the name *Catalina Express*.

SANTA CATALINA ISLAND COMPANY

The retirement of Malcolm Renton and the death of Philip Wrigley only two years later, prompted William Wrigley, the chairman of the SCICo Board's Executive Committee, to appoint Claude Brooks president. Brooks had sound working relationships with both Philip K. and William Wrigley. Between 1977 and 1985, Brooks worked closely with William Wrigley to reshape the SCICo management team and business plan. Together they provided the leadership and continuity needed during this transitional time.

Claude Brooks

THE 1980s

During the 1980s, Two Harbors added its historic first one-room schoolhouse and acquired its own postal service. Catalina Express started daily boat service to Catalina Island with an increase in the fleet, including an expanded and modernized Catalina Holiday boat service from Newport Beach to a new 15,000 sq. ft. freight terminal at Pebbly Beach.

In 1988, after 9 years at SCICo and three years as vice president, Paxson Offield was appointed president of SCICo. Mr. Offield became the first president and member of the Wrigley-Offield family since the 1919 acquisition of SCICo by William Wrigley Jr. to reside full time in Avalon.

In March of 1988, SCICo initiated a comprehensive planning study that included a series of visitor surveys and community workshops aimed at shedding light on unmet visitor and community needs. From the visitors' perspective, one of the main concerns was a lack of sufficient quality hotel rooms. From the community perspective, issues included: housing, a community center, traffic congestion, fire station, city hall, and number one on the list, a larger grocery store.

The SCICo 15-Year Plan was created to meet the needs of both groups. One of the cornerstones of the plan was the concept of a high-quality resort in Descanso Cove. Another critical element was

provision of affordable housing. Responding to this critical need, the City of Avalon acquired Eucalyptus Hill from SCICo for an 80-unit affordable housing project. Within one year of completion of the project, the complex was fully occupied.

SCICo Exec Management Team, 1985 - Back row, left to right, William Wrigley, Paxson Offield, Darrell Mulvihill, Ronald Doutt, Claude Brooks, Raiford Roberts. Front row, left to right, Kris Williamson, Rudy Piltch, and Erika Kingett.

WILMINGTON TRANSPORTATION COMPANY CHANGES OWNERSHIP

(Excerpts from a letter dated August 27, 1998 to all Santa Catalina Island Company employees from Paxson H. Offield, President & CEO – great-grandson of William Wrigley Jr.)

Nearly 80 years ago, when my great-grandfather acquired the Santa Catalina Island Company, he also acquired its wholly owned subsidiary, the Wilmington Transportation Company (WTCo). WTCo was established in 1884, primarily to help vessels off-load supplies destined for the fledgling Pueblo of Los Angeles. It is now the oldest, continuously operated company in the L.A. Harbor.

Over the years WTCo experienced numerous changes, but it always had a "core" ship assist function. From the late 1880's to the early 1960's, WTCo was also the principal provider of passenger and freight transportation services to Santa Catalina Island using, primarily, the large and, ultimately, inefficient steamers, *S.S. Catalina and S.S. Avalon.*

In the 1960's, my great uncle, Philip Wrigley, made what was then considered by some to be a controversial decision, and that was to have WTCo exit the business of carrying passengers and freight to Catalina. He knew that what was needed was smaller, faster vessels on a more frequent time schedule. His decision created the conditions for others to step forward with innovative ideas, and Catalina now benefits from perhaps the best passenger carrying services it has ever had. This change also gave SCICo the ability to better focus on the "product" the visitor was coming to see (Avalon and Santa Catalina Island). As a consequence, our island community has more to offer to visitors, and we have a much better year-round economy. In short, the visiting public seems to be better served as a result of this change, both in terms of transportation options and things to do and see once they arrive.

After leaving the passenger carrying business, WTCo returned to its roots as a first rate tugboat company, expanding and upgrading its fleet into twin screw tugboats. In the early 1980's, in response to increased competitive pressures and in an effort to sustain profitability in the face of shrinking margins, another change was adopted when WTCo entered the bunker barge business. Despite this relatively bold move, fundamental changes were altering WTCo's marketplace and an aggressive response was required. We, therefore, invested millions of dollars in new equipment and improvements to our existing fleet, increased levels of insurance nearly twenty fold in response to new legislation and customer demands, pursued new technology and refocused our marketing efforts. Despite these efforts and notwithstanding the dedication, loyalty and hard work of our crews and management teams, WTCo continued to struggle in the 1990's.

Those struggles are chiefly a function of what is going on in the marketplace. Ships are now much bigger and governmental rules more complex. In this environment, customers increasingly, and understandably, expect tug companies to provide the best available technology – which means tractor tugs that cost upward of $6 million each. So the number of ships calling on ports is static, our equipment costs are higher and the prices ship owners are willing to pay have remained flat. Further, the Oil Pollution Act of 1990 forced significant increases to our ocean liability

insurance costs, and bunker prices in L.A. led to a significant lowering of the volume of oil bunkers sold in L.A. and Long Beach. Couple this with the very onerous penalties in the event of an oil spill, which could not only put WTCo out of business but bankrupt the entire company, and you have a very challenging and risky business environment. These forces have impacted all major U.S. ports – not just L.A. Harbor. These market dynamics have resulted in a major consolidation of the American ship assist industry over the past decade. Small tug companies up and down the coast have had to go out of business or sell out, sometimes at a loss. Larger, multi-port tug companies are better able to respond to changing needs and the increase in regulatory oversight.

Despite our efforts to deal aggressively with these changing conditions, it became increasingly clear (just as it must have been similarly clear to my great uncle in the 1960's) that a change was necessary for the benefit of our core businesses on Santa Catalina Island. We reluctantly agreed that it was in the best, long-term interest of SCICo and WTCo to consider a sale of WTCo, if the right buyer were to come our way and we were to receive a fair price.

It was within this backdrop that we were recently approached by Foss Maritime Company, which, through a wholly owned subsidiary, wished to acquire WTCo… Like WTCo, Foss is over 100 years old, but it has its roots in the Pacific Northwest. Foss has grown to become one of the West Coast's most successful ship assist, ocean towing and bunker barging companies. Foss exhibited a sincere and unique interest in WTCo's equipment, its customers and its employees. After negotiations, we reached an agreement in principle to sell all of the outstanding shares of WTCo, which were owned by SCICo, to Foss Maritime Company…

It is expected that the sale of WTCo will close on September 30, 1998. Our WTCo friends will be missed, but their professional opportunities, I feel, are greater now with a large maritime company with operations in numerous ports than they would have been under our continued

stewardship. Similarly, our customers should be better served by a firm with far more in the way of maritime resources than we have to offer…

I salute all of our WTCo friends and thank them for their hard work and dedication. I also wanted everyone on Santa Catalina Island to understand, and hopefully appreciate, the background and the amount of forethought that went into making this every difficult decision.

Sincerely,

Paxson H. Offield

President & CEO

Santa Catalina Island Company

DR. STEVEN B. SAMPLE, President – University of Southern California.

Bill Wrigley was already a member of the USC Board of Trustees when I became president of the university in 1991. From then until his untimely passing in 1999, he and I enjoyed a warm friendship. In many ways the model of a university trustee, he had a unique vision for teaching and research in the area of environmental studies, and he was willing to invest generously to make that vision a reality. His dedicated commitment, his deliberate counsel, and his wise guidance advanced the university's mission tremendously.

When I think of Bill, the word that immediately comes to mind is "stewardship." He believed that the world and its institutions were sacred trusts that he was to maintain and improve for the generations to come. He was a steward of USC, helping to lead it during a time of rapid advancement. He was a steward of the Wm. Wrigley Jr. Co., making it one of the world's greatest companies. And he was a devoted steward of Santa Catalina Island, ensuring that his family's vision for the island and its environment was carried forward.

All of us at USC are grateful for Bill Wrigley's generosity with his time, his talent, and his fortune. His legacy lives on in the USC Wrigley Institute for Environmental Studies, where generations of scientists and students are studying and learning from a uniquely preserved environment.

RONALD C. DOUTT, President and COO of the Santa Catalina Island Company.

There are numerous themes and threads to the Wrigley family's legacy of leadership. Heading the list is their personal commitment and active involvement as both owners and officers of the Santa Catalina Island Company. The second common trait that transcends generations is their high ethical standards, professionalism and class. Next is the family's recognition of the need to select, nurture and encourage a non-family

management group which appreciates and effectively executes the family's vision. Another common thread which has linked the various generations of Wrigleys is an unwavering commitment to the betterment of the environment.

Early on in my career with SCICo, William Wrigley sent signals that he was working toward a time when most Catalina-related decision-making would occur in Avalon. Shortly after being hired he advised me that "Packy (Offield) will be your mentor. Welcome aboard." In fact, Packy, Alison (Wrigley-Rusack), Mr. Wrigley and Mr. Wrigley's sister Blanny have all "mentored" me by demonstrating in both deed and in word how to gracefully discharge the awesome responsibility "being a Wrigley" (or, more accurately as respects me, "working for and representing the Wrigleys") has in the context of one's role with Santa Catalina Island. Let me elaborate by fleshing out a little more fully what it is, in my opinion that make Bill Wrigley and Packy Offield so special.

Mr. Wrigley was an officer and director of the Santa Catalina Island Company for 35 years and never took a dime in salary. Unlike his father and grandfather, William Wrigley attended and graduated from college (Yale). He both embraced and practiced a more "cerebral" approach to management. He understood the value of high quality management information and the need to make the investments needed to supply such on a timely basis.

He was also a very savvy advertising man, understood the value of building consensus, and ran his businesses on a fiscally sound basis. To this day, SCICo is still not burdened with debt. In the 14 years I knew and worked with Mr. Wrigley, the traits that are most vivid are his dedication and hard work. His mind was constantly on the business tasks at hand. No one at any of his far-flung enterprises worked harder or for longer hours than Mr. Wrigley. He led by example but he was also very fair.

On each of his trips to Catalina, Packy and I would sit down with Mr. Wrigley to go over the latest monthly financial statements. During these sessions it was abundantly clear that Mr. Wrigley's recall of the intricate interrelationships of our operations was uncanny. That attention to detail manifested itself in many other ways – by being involved with the choice of colors for a new glass bottom boat, in reviewing advertising layout and copy, by checking the math in budgets and other financial documents, by reading everything that was placed before him for signature, and even by his obsession with neatness. None of this involvement was micro-managing; rather it was his effort to impart to his management team how he thought and to underscore his, and his family's management philosophy. Mr. Wrigley was always more of a teacher than a boss and he was very effective in that tutorial role. I learned much from that man.

ROSE ELLEN GARDNER, former President and CEO of the Santa Catalina Island Conservancy.

In remembrance of Mr. William Wrigley, I would like to share with you the words I shared with those who attended his memorial service in the Casino Theatre on Santa Catalina Island on March 29:

"I am honored to have been asked to say a few words this afternoon about a man whom I have known, admired and respected for the past 25 years – Mr. William Wrigley.

"As a Benefactor Member of the Conservancy, Mr. Wrigley took very seriously the responsibility of his membership. However, his dedication to the organization and to Catalina Island went far beyond the membership duties written in our bylaws. His love for the island and his commitment to ensuring that the major portion of it would be preserved for us and for future generations to enjoy was evident in his opinions and his actions. On more than once occasion he looked me straight in the eye, as only Mr. Wrigley could do, and said, 'Rose Ellen, it's vitally important that we make sure the Conservancy has sufficient resources to continue to operate in the event some unknown catastrophe occurs.' As you can tell, these

words are etched in my memory, and I certainly will not forget them as they have already served us well.

"A few years ago, my husband, Dave, and I and two of our close friends visited Chicago for a long weekend. None of us had ever visited there before, and we had a wonderful time seeing the sights. On our last day, we were invited to tour the Wrigley Building. This was a treat for all of us, but especially for me as growing up in Avalon, I had heard about it all my life and always hoped someday to see it in person. Not only were we treated to a tour of the building, but Mr. Wrigley took time out of his busy day to personally show us their newly-remodeled conference room complete with a demonstration of all of the latest electronic equipment. As usual, his careful attention to detail was evident in each and every aspect of the room.

"Mr. Wrigley loved small animals. On one occasion, several of us from the Conservancy were invited to join other guests from the mainland for dinner at his home, Casa del Monte. The visiting guests belonged to an environmental organization, and Mr. Wrigley thought they might enjoy seeing an example of Catalina's wildlife. so he also invited us to bring the little Catalina Island fox, which immediately curled up in his arms and spent the entire evening in his lap. When it was time to leave, it was a toss up as to who was the most disappointed, the fox or Mr. Wrigley. We all had a wonderful evening that night, but we were never sure if it was our company Mr. Wrigley wanted or the fox's.

"When my own father passed away five years ago, I received a personal letter from Mr. Wrigley which I still have today expressing his sympathy and condolences. The fact that he even knew of my father's passing, let alone that he took the time from his busy schedule to write, left a lasting impression on me.

"It is true, we have lost a friend, a supporter, a guidance counselor and a lover of nature, however, the examples he set for us of honesty, attention to detail, good business principles and kindness remain with us forever…"

PART FOUR
WRIGLEY FAMILY TRADITIONS

William Wrigley, Jr. riding his favorite horse, Bingo, in Avalon.

≈ LOVE OF HORSES ≈

Horses and riding were always a big part of Wrigley family life at Catalina. William Wrigley, Jr., had worked with horses and wagons during his boyhood in Pennsylvania, and he maintained a fine stable in Avalon when he was in his sixties. During the 1920s, he was often seen riding the roads and trails around Avalon on his cherished horse, Bingo.

El Rancho Escondido, riding arena and tack rooms.

Helen Atwater Wrigley posing on Sheik and Deedie watching from the side.

Philip Wrigley inherited his father's love of horses. After establishing the beautiful El Rancho Escondido atop a ridge in the rugged interior of the island, Philip and his family spent many happy months in the company of their beloved island horses. There were many adventures that would bring back a lifetime of memories, later shared by Philip's eldest daughter, Blanny, and other members of the Wrigley family.

Blanny recalls that the first ranch house at El Rancho Escondido (now the manager's home) had two bedrooms and a sitting room linked together by a covered porch. Blanny and Deedie used to quietly leave their room in the morning to ride horses – careful not to wake up dad and "munna". One morning, unable to get their door open, the girls climbed out the window and walked around to the porch to investigate. Much to their surprise, a buffalo cow was lying on the porch, pressed up against their bedroom door for warmth.

Alison Wrigley Rusack riding Adara, daughter of Catalina bred champion Adibiyez, at Shark Harbor with husband Geoff.

Bill Wrigley riding at the ranch with grandson Hunter Rusack.

El Rancho Escondido living quarters.

Philip in the hills of Catalina.

In the early years of the ranch, there were many feral horses on the island, the descendants of stagecoach horses that were turned loose and bred with wild horses left on the island by the early Spanish explorers. It was decided to round up these animals, but the ranch horses couldn't keep up with the feral herd and it always got away. Philip Wrigley and John Fouts, a rodeo rider who worked on the ranch for many years, hatched a plan to catch one of the wild horses and break him to be used in rounding up the herd. John caught a beautiful red roan they named "Buzz." It could not handle a heavy bit and halter, so Fouts rode Buzz bareback with a rope lead at his head. The plan was a success. Philip bred some of the feral horses they were able to capture with the Arabians of El Rancho Escondido; the offspring proved to be truly outstanding and beautiful horses.

Paul Harper, Blanny's godfather, was close to the Wrigley family for many years. William Wrigley Jr. brought Mr. Harper along as a tutor for Philip when he took his family around the world. The teacher, fluent in Arabic and other languages, began to give the horses born at El Rancho Escondido Arabic names, beginning with Bakir, which is "one," through Saba, "seven." After Harper's death, the practice ended. No one at the ranch knew how to continue counting in Arabic.

Blanny recalled the names of many favorite mounts used by the family on the island through the years. Philip Wrigley rode Kaaba or Big Boy. Favorites of the children included Kadir, Trigger, Judy, Star, and Tom Thumb. Deedie Wrigley went on to breed Arabians as an adult.

Philip Wrigley was very "hands-on" in the development of the ranch property. He used an Oliver tractor to build and upgrade roads at El Rancho Escondido. He came home one afternoon and announced to the family that he'd "had a close call today." He had taken the tractor onto the steep side of a hill where it slipped and rolled all the way to the bottom of the canyon. Luckily, he jumped off before it tipped over. The tractor landed treads down, and Mr. Wrigley simply climbed back on and finished his day's work. In view of incidents like these, it is no wonder that through the years, people often asked Philip's sister Dorothy Offield, if he was still alive when they greeted her.

Wild Bison herd on Catalina Island.

Shipping horses by steamer. All these photos show Jack White leading Kaaba into the padded stall.

The Wrigley family's love affair with horses was also evident in the way they transported their treasured equines. Padded crates were made to transport the horses to and from Santa Catalina Island aboard the *SS Catalina*, the big white steamship, and Wilmington Transportation Company barges. The sides of the crates were assembled, the horse was gently moved between them and the ends were attached.

Philip Wrigley had what was probably the first horse trailer built especially for his horse, Kaaba, so that he could drive the horse to the ranch from the steamer or barge instead of riding him. The trailer had no top, and Philip was cautious to keep dust and debris out of the horse's eyes during transport. He asked Edward H. Bohlin who, was considered "Saddlemaker and Silversmith to the Stars" and made saddles for the Wrigleys at the ranch, to make custom leather goggles for Kaaba to wear in the open trailer, up the summit to the ranch and back down to the boat. No effort was spared for the comfort of these beloved horses.

Valencia, the donkey, dressed up and ready to pull her new Sicilian Donkey Cart, a gift from John Mitchell to the Wrigley family. Ranch Manager Jack White's Australian Shepherd, Queen, is ready for the ride.

Deedie on her horse named Jimmy, Blanny, Grandpa Bert Atwater on the white horse Tom Thumb, and Gan Gan.

The Wrigley family sent Santa Catalina Island entries to the Tournament of Roses parades in Pasadena, California on New Year's Day in the 1930s. Frenchy Small, who ran the livery stable in Avalon for the Santa Catalina Island Company, drove an elaborately decorated island-based stagecoach and horses in the parade. The horses were transported to and from Santa Catalina on the barge along with the massive coach. Ranch manager, Jack White and ranch-hand John Fouts went along to make sure it was smooth sailing for both cargo and animals. Frenchy had been taught to drive the six-horse stagecoach by former island owner Captain William Banning.

The Wrigleys had a great love for animals in general and truly cared about their well being. Valencia, a donkey, lived for more than 40 years on the island at El Rancho Escondido. Philip Wrigley said that she had

two gears – stand still and run away. No matter what was done to the little donkey, if she didn't want to go, she would stand there with her head down. As soon as Valencia picked up her head however, she was off and running. There was no way to stop her until she "ran out of gas." The best that could be hoped for was to try and steer her with a rope harness, since she didn't use a bit.

Blanny and Deedie tried the "carrot-on-a-stick" trick, attaching a carrot on a string to the end of a long buggy whip. Valencia grabbed the carrot and took off running with the girls holding on for dear life. When Valencia tired, the girls were able to steer her safely back to the ranch. Philip's granddaughter, Misdee Wrigley, underwrote the donkey's expenses for food and care at the Middle Ranch until Valencia expired not long ago.

Philip on Khorshed with his parade saddle and all the dressings.

William "Bill" Wrigley was a great lover of horses. He put on horse shows at his large custom stables at Lake Geneva, Wisconsin every July 4th. Bill and Julie were also very involved in national Arabian horse shows as sponsors and benefactors. Bill's daughter Alison has many fond memories of her time on the Island. She shared the following story at her father's memorial service on Catalina in May 1999.

"As a child, I eagerly anticipated our trips to Catalina. Among the many reasons I loved coming here, perhaps the most important to me was the special time I got to spend with my father.

After surviving the seemingly endless curves (and my inevitable carsickness) as we made our way to the ranch in a VW bus, Dad and I would head down to the barn as soon as we could and saddle up. For a little girl infatuated with horses, escaping the confines of Chicago to ride the hills of Catalina with the father I adored was as close to heaven as I could imagine.

Not that it was all idyllic. Dad was never one to follow established trails, and I often found myself balanced on the edge of some cliff, holding two fidgety Arabians, as he hacked his way through the brush with his knife. However, no matter how impossible the obstacles we encountered seemed, Dad had invariably thought up several plans of how to get through, and we would always make it back somehow – usually just in time to relish one of his (and my) favorite meals of macaroni and cheese with cut-up hot dogs.

Unbeknownst to me at the time, I learned a lot about courage, patience, and perseverance on those escapades, (not to mention the importance of thinking ahead!)

Like his grandfather and father, Dad cared deeply for Catalina, and spent countless hours working with so many trying to do what would be best for it, and its residents and friends. Though it may not have been obvious because of his quiet and unassuming manner, he also cared about the people of Catalina.

Dad loved the Old West, its art, cowboys, wide-open spaces and small towns. Catalina and Avalon personified much of that to him."

Goat and cattle were used in the roping demonstrations, as seen in both photos above, and below.

Drawing of ranch manager Jack White. The inscription reads "To one of the liveliest gals I ever knew Jack."

Bill's son, "Bill Jr.," now has the Lake Geneva barn and is raising polo ponies. Bill Jr.'s daughter, Kristin, is turning out to be an excellent rider at the age of nine, it's in her blood, just like the rest of the Wrigleys.

The Wrigley family's history of horse breeding and training is carried on today by Misdee Wrigley, daughter of Dorothy (Deedie) Wrigley Chauncey. Misdee owns and operates Hillcroft Farm in the Bluegrass Region of Kentucky. Hillcroft, named for the long-time Wrigley country home at Lake Geneva, specializes in both saddlebreds and Hackney horses.

A large room in the barn at Hillcroft houses an impressive collection of family memorabilia. A custom-made western saddle used by Ms. Wrigley's grandmother, Helen, enjoys a place of honor. Several antique carriages in pristine condition are also displayed here. An elegant 1898 Station Brougham, featuring an enclosed compartment for passengers and an outside seat for the driver, was built for William Wrigley Jr., Misdee's great-grandfather. Another carriage known as a "vis-à-vis," which was popular in the 18th and 19th centuries, was used by Ada Wrigley, her great-grandmother. Passengers rode facing each other in this small, sporty conveyance.

Jack White, John Fouts and Frenchy Small sitting on a barge.

Taking goats and horses used in roping demonstrations back to mainland on the barge. Onlookers in the background at the left are Olive Atwater Getz, Helen Wrigley's sister; Bill and Helen Wrigley; and Philip Wrigley with his camera.

Philip riding Bakir with a saddle he acquired in Arabia.

Philip on Kaaba.

Misdee Wrigley also has fond memories of Santa Catalina Island. She maintains a home in Avalon, and visits when she can. Fourth-generation descendant of William Wrigley Jr., she deeply loves horses – and the island as well.

Misdee's sister, Helen, also participates in showing Saddlebred horses and Hackney ponies when she is not traveling as an accomplished author and publisher. Blanny's daughter, Blanny Avalon is a longtime rancher, riding instructor and horse show competitor.

Reverence For The Environment
A Brief History Of The USC Wrigley Institute

Unloading road material from barge as construction starts at Little Fisherman Cove.

Dormitory construction at the Philip K. Wrigley Marine Science Center on Santa Catalina Island.

USC classrooms, laboratory, and residential construction for the Wrigley Marine Science Center.

Excerpts from
A BRIEF HISTORY OF THE USC WRIGLEY INSTITUTE
By Professor Anthony Michaels,
Director of the Marine Science Center

In 1965, Philip K. Wrigley deeded 5.5 acres of land from the Santa Catalina Island Company to USC to create a marine science center at Two Harbors. A $500,000 grant was obtained from the National Science Foundation and that, along with some private contributions and some University funds, made it possible to build the laboratories at Big Fisherman's Cove. In 1967, Philip Wrigley provided USC with an additional eight acres adjacent to the newly built facility. He also began making annual contributions of $20,000 to $25,000 per year for upkeep. By 1975, the Wrigley family's commitment widened with the gifting of Santa Catalina Island Company stock from shares controlled by Philip Wrigley and his sister, Mrs. Dorothy Offield. The following year additional SCI Company stock was given to USC, bringing the value of the University's holdings to $7,210,000. Upon Philip Wrigley's death in 1977, USC became the beneficiary of his remaining shares of preferred (non voting) SCI Company stock.

Upon his father's passing, William Wrigley asked then USC President, Norman Topping to join the Santa Catalina Island Company Board of Directors in 1977, beginning a policy of membership for the incumbent University President that continues today. The following year, the Wrigley family home at Mt. Ada in Avalon was deeded to USC as a site for the activities of the Institute for Marine and Coastal Studies.

William Wrigley began making regular annual contributions of $250,000 to the Marine Science Center beginning in 1985 with his wife, Julie Wrigley. In recognition of his support, the University offered to name the Institute at their designation in 1990. He chose to name it for his father, and thus the Institute's Catalina Island facility became the Philip K. Wrigley Marine Science Center.

Philip and Helen Wrigley meet Will Foreman, pilot of "Deep View" sub.

Philip and Helen Wrigley help escort the submarine out of the hanger.

William Wrigley's regular annual contributions continued and became increasingly generous. When the University approached him in July of 1995 about a five-phase $60 million plan to expand the research and educational capabilities of the Marine Center, he provided an initial $5 million gift as start-up capital. The plan outlined how a $30 million Wrigley family investment, matched by a like amount from USC, would create an internationally recognized institute based on Catalina Island. With his first commitment to this project, William Wrigley helped create the USC Wrigley Institute for Environmental Studies, the first phase of a programmatic expansion of the Philip K. Wrigley Marine Science Center. At that time, William Wrigley made it clear that his future investment in the project would be based upon acceptable progress by the University and the Institute.

The gift provided for a $1.25 million laboratory and classroom renovation at the Catalina Island facility as well as for an endowed chair ($1.5 million), for an Institute directorship ($1.5 million), a transportation fund ($450,000) and programmatic support to create a multi-disciplinary research and teaching program in environmental studies. This enabling gift was matched by an $8.7 million commitment of USC resources in the first phase. This landmark investment catapulted the Marine Science Center on Catalina from a minor role in USC's marine science program and a destination for visiting faculty, to status as the centerpiece of a multi-disciplinary environmental research and teaching center.

By early 1997, the first expansion phase was complete. Professor Anthony Michaels had been appointed as director and was overseeing a full slate of short-term summer courses, a renewed Catalina Semester, and spinning up new research projects on a range of topics including environmental risk and business decisions, environmental economics, biological oceanography and marine biology. Pleased by this progress, William Wrigley provided an additional $5 million gift to begin phase two. In that same year the first Wrigley Institute Advisory Board was established.

Christening of the Naval Undersea Research and Development Center submersible "Deep View."

"Deep View" submarine being lowered into the ocean.

The submarine "Deep View" moving from its hanger to the ocean on its first dive.

Beginning in the spring of 1998, the Wrigley Institute was able to offer a full-semester program that now included both a biology track and an environmental studies track and was beginning an ambitious telepresence marine science education program for the Los Angeles and Long Beach Unified School Districts.

In 1999, William Wrigley made a third gift of $5 million to the Wrigley Institute. The funds for programmatic development have been especially valuable, leading to large government sponsored projects and innovative programs that have become self-sustaining models for USC. These resources have funded the research faculty, project assistants, travel, equipment and salaries necessary to launch new projects. Fellowships have been equally valuable. The USC Wrigley Institute is one of only a handful of marine and environmental science institutions to have a dedicated postdoctoral fellowship program.

By 2001, the research agenda had expanded so dramatically that the Wrigley Institute was named the number two organization in the nation in terms of National Science Foundation funded marine biology research. (Woods Hole Oceanographic Institute is number one.)

Among the research projects underway were studies of: population genetics of marine organisms, with an emphasis on applications to conservation biology; population genetic structure in striped Marlin (funded in part by Paxson Offield). More than ever, the Wrigley Institute was a prime destination for marine researchers around the world.

The educational outreach efforts had grown to include a summer school program "young women in science," and the Catalina Island Education Consortium (made up of representatives from the Catalina Island Conservancy, Catalina Island Marine Institute, Catalina Museum and USC Sea Grant"), an after-school enrichment program for local Catalina Island 4th – 6th graders.

William Wrigley's gifts, since 1995, totaled $16 million. USC also has invested substantial amounts of the College's funds to ensure that the institute today lives up to the scale of the commitments made in 1995 to William Wrigley.

When he died, discussions with William Wrigley about providing $15 million for Phase IV and V were still progressing. His initial response had been that his further investment would come from his estate including a $1 million insurance policy through Texaco (this was received).

Arizona Biltmore 1956

Atwater Girl, Dorse Offield with Packy & Jimmy, Blanny H, Will H, John H, Phil H, George R, Helen R.

DOROTHY WRIGLEY OFFIELD
DAUGHTER OF WILLIAM WRIGLEY, JR.

Dorothy Wrigley Offield

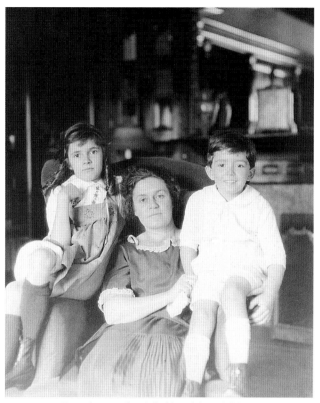

*Dorothy Wrigley Offield and her children,
Betty and Wrigley "Bud".*

Dorothy Wrigley was born in 1889. She was the first child of Ada and William Wrigley Jr., "Da" as she was known to family and close friends was very close to her brother Philip Knight, particularly in their later years. She married James R. Offield and had two children, Ada Elizabeth and Wrigley. Dorothy's husband James, an attorney, was a director of the Wm Wrigley Jr. Company from 1911 until his death in 1964.

Throughout the Wrigley family's early time on Santa Catalina Island, Dorothy Wrigley Offield enjoyed the natural beauty of the magic isle and its people. In 1975, Dorothy, along with her brother Philip and his wife Helen, deeded 42,135 acres to the Santa Catalina Island Conservancy to ensure the protection of the majority of the island that was so special to her.

Wrigley "Bud" Offield.

*Wrigley "Bud" Offield and Edna Jean
on their honeymoon at Catalina in 1941.*

Continuing the tradition of involvement in the "family" business, Dorothy's son Wrigley "Bud" Offield joined the Wm Wrigley Jr. Company as an employee in 1940, retiring as Vice President of Advertising in 1966. He then served as a board member until 1982 when he was made an honorary director. Bud also served as a director of the Santa Catalina Island Company as well as being president and director of the Offield Family Foundation. Bud Offield also served as the President of the Arizona Biltmore hotel and developed the renowned Arizona Biltmore Fashion Park.

Bud Offield, like Philip Wrigley, had a great love for flying. He owned and operated a 290 horsepower Stinson airplane that was fully equipped for instrument, night and long cross-country flying. On December 11, 1941 Bud sent a letter to the Army Air Corp, offering his services as a pilot to ferry aircraft on a volunteer basis. The fact that he had to wear corrective lenses at all times kept him from being able to enlist as a pilot but Bud wanted to serve his country – even as a volunteer in a "desk" job connected with aviation.

Bud's wife, Edna Jean nee Headley Offield was also known for her involvement in charitable organizations. "eddi" as she was known by family and close friends was also well known for her artistic creativity and being an outstanding benefactor and advocate for the arts and culture in Northern Michigan. eddi, like many other Wrigley family members, loved planes and had been a pilot.

Wrigley Offield passed away on July 17, 1991 at the age of 74. Edna Jean Offield passed away on March 31, 2001 at the age of 82. They were the proud parents of a daughter, Dorsse and two sons, James S. and Paxson H. Offield.

❧ PAXSON H. OFFIELD ❧
GREAT-GRANDSON OF WILLIAM WRIGLEY JR.
CHAIRMAN AND CEO OF SANTA CATALINA ISLAND COMPANY

Paxson H. Offield has a home in Avalon. Like his father before him, he attended the Catalina Island School for Boys at Toyon Bay from 1968 to 1970. He returned after graduation from Denver University to teach there. Packy was the second Catalina Island School for Boys alumnus to return as a faculty member.

Packy was the first Wrigley family member to live on the island full time (and, incidentally, was also the first Santa Catalina Island Company President to live in Avalon full time). Because his father was both a Director of the Santa Catalina Island Company and President of the Arizona Biltmore, throughout his younger years Packy's family would split time at spring break between Catalina and Phoenix.

Today Mr. Offield is CEO and Chairman of the Board of the Santa Catalina Island Company. He succeeded Bill Wrigley as Santa Catalina Island Company's President in 1988. Packy's efforts have been directed towards creating a year-round economy, providing visitors with a quality experience, and increasing the financial health of both the City of Avalon and the Santa Catalina Island Company. To better understand how to best proceed with this vision, Packy got involved with the City of Avalon's Planning Commission, serving in the early 1980s and was its Chairman when Avalon's Local Coastal Plan was adopted. Recognizing the need for a vital and active business community, he became President of the Avalon/Catalina Island Chamber of Commerce as it redefined itself into the model tourism and business support group that it is today.

Packy's specific focus during his tenure with the Chamber was on how to improve the "Undiscovered Season," the period of time between September and June. He directly helped to extend Avalon's tourism season by personally underwriting and/or making available Santa Catalina Island Company venues for events that were designed to attract visitors to the island in spring and fall. As shared by Ronald Doutt, the current President and COO of the SCICo, "The emergence and early success of the Jazz Trax Festival, the Plein Air Painters Show, the Catalina Marathon, the Silent Film benefit, the Blues Festival and numerous tag and release fishing tournaments are to a large degree due to Packy – a fact that he does not, and will not, publicize."

He is also a Benefactor Member of the Santa Catalina Island

Paxson H. Offield.

Conservancy, who shares responsibility for overseeing its assets and electing the board of directors, as well as being a Member of the Board of Directors. He was the Conservancy's first Chairman of the Board.

Paxson also serves on numerous boards around the country. He is Chairman of the Catalina Seabass Fund, a Past President of the Tuna Club, and a Board Member of the Billfish Foundation. He is Chairman of the Peregrine Fund, and sits on the USC Wrigley Institute for Environmental Studies Board of Advisors. He also is a Director of the Sheriff's Youth Foundation. Paxson is President and a Board Member of the Offield Family Foundation and President of the Blue Maple River Company, a Michigan corporation.

Packy, as he is known to family and friends, has a passion and commitment to conservation not only through his activities with many environmental groups but especially in his work with the Billfish Foundation. Addressing the global problem of the dwindling population of broadbill, marlin and other billfish, Packy has devoted countless hours and has been a tireless benefactor for these important organizations.

Packy and his wife Susan reside in Avalon. He has three children – Chase, Kelsey, Calen and stepson, Rex - of whom he is very proud.

ADA BLANCHE (BLANNY) WRIGLEY SCHREINER
DAUGHTER OF PHILIP K. WRIGLEY

Ada Blanche Wrigley Schreiner

Once, when Blanny, sister Deedie and ranch foreman Jack White were riding down to Empire Landing, they spotted fishermen poachers on a beach packing off a dead steer they had shot. White shouted to the girls, "get outta here fast!" and they rode to safety over a ridge but not before one of the poachers fired a rifle at them. Jack, gun drawn, raced down the mountain to the beach and took the poachers into custody, transporting them single-handedly in the fishing boat to the Avalon City Jail.

Ada Blanche Wrigley Schreiner with Husband Charles, granddaughter Samantha Catalina, and her beloved Irish Wolf Hound Donegal Glocca Morra.

B lanny recalls that the family spent two to three months at Avalon each winter or spring. They would arrive as early as February and depart in April or May. There were sometimes shorter summer visits. They lived at Casa del Monte and the children had a resident tutor, Mrs. Swett. Blanny, her sister Deedie, and brother Bill all grew to love the mountains, canyons and beaches of Santa Catalina Island.

For the Wrigley children, leaving Chicago in the grip of winter and traveling to Santa Catalina off the coast of southern California was an exciting change. There they could hike, beachcomb and ride every day.

On other, more peaceful horseback jaunts around the island, Blanny Wrigley was able to observe the island's natural beauty. As a girl of nine years of age, she had begun writing poems detailing her observations. She has published two books, One Poet's Legacy: A Gift of Love and Reflections on My Life with the Irish Wolfhound.

Patricia Anne Moore, former Director/Curator of the Catalina Island Museum shared this story about Blanny:

When it was announced that the William Wrigley Jr. home on Mt. Ada was to be transferred to the USC Marine Science Institute for use as a conference center, the Museum Society received permission to conduct a tour of the home for its annual membership drive. The home, which still contained much of the original furniture used by the family, was a historical gem and aroused a great deal of curiosity. Mr. and Mrs. Philip Wrigley were strong supporters of the Museum and Mrs. Helen Wrigley and her daughters occasionally attended Museum Board meetings. Dale Eisenhut, superintendent of the Casino Building where the Museum is located, was on the Board at the time and he suggested that we invite Ada Blanche "Blanny" Wrigley Schreiner to be our hostess for the occasion. To our delight, she accepted and traveled to Avalon especially for the occasion.

Blanny arrived at Mt. Ada shortly before the tour was about to begin, wearing a simple but elegant print dress. She had a trim figure, good legs, and dainty feet showcased in dress sandals with modest heels. We had thought that she would probably sit somewhere comfortable so people could chat with her, but she stationed herself near the entrance to the parlor and began to greet the guests. She welcomed each person with a friendly smile, a handshake, and a few words. A steady stream of 420 people visited Mt. Ada that day and Blanny greeted them all with the same warmth—she stood there for hours.

I was helping coordinate the event so I moved around quite a bit. Occasionally, I would glance her way and see her gallantly holding her position. At times one foot would rise ever so slightly and flex and rotate discreetly for a few seconds before returning to its place. A little later, the other foot would execute the same maneuver. I cherish that memory of a gracious lady with tired feet. I took it as a sign of her extraordinary character, her sense of duty and her pride in her family's role in shaping Catalina Island. Her continued support of the Island and the Museum has confirmed my judgment

Blanny married William John Hagenah, Jr. of Glencoe, Illinois in January of 1943. They had four children: Will, Phil, Blanny and John. They divorced in 1962.

Blanny and her husband, the Rev. Charles Schreiner reside in Washington state and at Hamilton Cove, Avalon. "Charlie" is a retired Episcopalian priest, who served with the Marines in World War II and was present at the battle of Okinawa. He is also a prolific writer, having published books and newspaper articles for more than 30 years. They have one son, Steve.

Ada Blanche Wrigley Schreiner has five children. Each of these people has developed their own legacy on Santa Catalina Island and is active in many aspects of the conservation and preservation of the magic isle as well as involvement in community activities.

Blanny's oldest son, William John Hagenah, recently retired from Bank One in the Chicago headquarters as Senior Vice President and long time head of the Private Banking and Trust department. He now, among many other things, serves as Chairman of the Board of the Chicago Botanic Garden, one of the largest in the United States, and as a Trustee of Rush University Medical Center in Chicago. Will has four daughters and currently six grandchildren.

Blanny's second son, Philip Wrigley Hagenah recently retired from 37 years in the commercial advertising production world and is currently serving on five boards, including the Advisory Board of the USC Wrigley Institute for Environmental Studies. He, his wife, Susan and their children hold a special place in their hearts for the island and visit as often as possible. Phil has three daughters and currently one grandson.

Her daughter, Blanny Avalon, worked for many years as an elementary and middle school teacher and a summer camp counselor. A long-time riding instructor and horse-show competitor, she has been active in the Catalina Island Pony Club, a charter member of the Las Caballeras Ladies' Catalina Riding Group, and has been a hands-on volunteer with the Santa Catalina Island Conservancy. She currently raises horses as well as her two children and splits her time between Avalon and Northern California.

Blanny's third son, John Hagenah is a successful, well-known architect working in the Chicago area creating designs and homes throughout the United States and Canada. He is also quite active in the Wilmette, Illinois Historical Society. John has a daughter and two sons.

Her fourth son, Steve Schreiner is a lawyer in Gig Harbor, Washington, specializing in real estate law and estate planning. He is very active as Vice President of the Catalina Island Museum Board and as a ranger for the Catalina Island Conservancy. He and his family also enjoy their home in Avalon.

DOROTHY (DEEDIE) WRIGLEY HANCOCK
DAUGHTER OF PHILIP K. WRIGLEY

Dorothy "Deedie" Wrigley born in 1926 was, sister Blanny told us, "very lively and outgoing, she loved people." From childhood Deedie had a great sense of humor. Blanny remembers one luncheon with Deedie and Helen Clark, a relative by marriage, at which the laughter kept rolling, fueled mostly by Deedie's quips. Blanny reported "my 'laugh' muscles were sore for days."

Deedie married George Rich in 1946. The couple had three children: Helen, Misdee, and George Thomas Rich. The childhood years of these children featured many happy visits to Catalina, where they divided their time between Casa del Monte in Avalon and El Rancho Escondido in the mountains of the interior.

El Rancho Escondido was a wonderful place to relax, but it was also a working ranch. Blanny remembers the occasion when she and Deedie were teens and their father Philip decided to create a roping arena south of the road running past the ranch headquarters. He had decided on a flat quarter-acre of land to use for the arena but it needed to be covered by sand to a depth of several inches. Deedie and Blanny were assigned, along with several members of the ranch crew, to take trucks to the beach at Little Harbor, shovel the truck beds full of sand and bring it back for spreading at the arena. A big job, which meant hard work, but a lot of fun, too.

Deedie's lifelong friend, Elizabeth Lawton, who grew up in Avalon, tells us of the many outings she and Deedie took with the island's equestrian club, The Vaqueros. Long nighttime rides of the 1930s and 1950s often had the Wrigley's El Rancho Escondido as a destination. There the riders would camp out and enjoy a meal under the stars with groups of Islander friends.

In the 1960s, Deedie was divorced from George Rich and later wed Tom Chauncey of Arizona. Mr. Chauncey was a lover of the western life and a long-time friend and business associate of Gene Autry. It was Deedie who acquainted him with Arabian horses and together, by the 1980s, they had built up their holdings of Arabians until they owned more than 260 of that beautiful breed. In 1984, after a marriage of more than twenty years, the couple parted.

Dorothy Wrigley Hancock with her prize-winning Arabians.

In 1990, Deedie married Dr. Richard Hancock. Dorothy (Deedie) Wrigley Hancock died in 1992, survived by her husband, Dr. Hancock, and her daughters Misdee and Helen. Her son, George Rich sadly died of a brain tumor at age forty. George had a successful career with the BBDO advertising agency in Chicago.

Of Deedie's three children, her oldest daughter Helen Rosberg is a successful and famous novelist best known for establishing and running a well-known publishing company (www.medallionpress.com), in addition to showing Saddlebred horses and Hackney ponies.

Deedie's second daughter, Misdee Wrigley is a former TV reporter, and now a Telly award winning documentary producer, also raising American Saddlebred horses, rare Hackney horses, and competes worldwide with antique carriages – "four-in-hand" – based in Kentucky at Hillcroft Farms. She has also been a longtime board member of the Santa Catalina Island Conservancy. Misdee and her sister Helen maintain a beautiful home in Avalon that was built by their mother.

WILLIAM (BILL JR.) WRIGLEY, JR.
SON OF WILLIAM (BILL) WRIGLEY

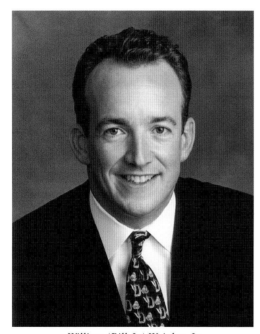

William (Bill Jr.) Wrigley, Jr.

William (Bill Jr.) Wrigley, Jr. took over the reins of the Wm. Wrigley Jr. Company after the death of his father in 1999. A graduate of Duke University with a Bachelor of Arts/Science Degree, he became a company Director in 1988, was Vice President from 1991 to 1999 and served as Assistant to the President from 1985 to 1992. He has been President and Chief Executive Officer since 1999 and was elected Chairman of the Board in 2004. There is no connection between the Wm. Wrigley Jr. Company, manufacturers of chewing gum, and the Santa Catalina Island Company. In an interview with *BusinessWeek* magazine, Bill Jr. described how he feels about being a part of the family legacy.

The thing I think you get with the right kind of family business is passion, people who are passionate about the business, who really care. In our case, obviously the family name is on the door, so we take great pride in that, and as a result take great pride in the whole company.

But even without the family name on the door, there's usually a very strong association with a family, and so it's more than just a job. It's not something you just walk out the door and don't think about...there's a certain passion and energy and commitment that goes with a family business.

Bill Jr. is also a member of the Evanston Hospital Board and a director of the Smucker Company. He is very proud of his three children, who also carry on the Wrigley family legacy.

William's oldest son, Philip Knight Wrigley is active in eye research, in-home theater design, and building. He and his wife Marilyn are long time residents on Arizona.

ALISON WRIGLEY RUSACK
DAUGHTER OF WILLIAM (BILL) WRIGLEY

William's daughter, Alison Wrigley Rusack, also has a passion for the family's legacy in Santa Catalina. A frequent visitor to the island since she was born, Alison has been told she was on a plane to Catalina and in the saddle in front of her father before she ever made it to a baby buggy. She has a great love for Catalina, and is involved with many aspects of the community.

Like her father before her, Alison holds majority voting ownership of the Santa Catalina Island Company, where she is also a member of the Board of Directors and an officer. She is a Benefactor member of the Santa Catalina Island Conservancy, and serves on the Advisory Board of the USC Wrigley Institute for Environmental Studies.

Alison and her husband, Geoffrey, own the highly-acclaimed Rusack Vineyards, a 6000-case winery located in the Santa Ynez Valley, near Santa Barbara, California. Alison graduated from Stanford University, after which she worked for 16 years in the entertainment industry in Southern California, most notably for Disney Consumer Products at their corporate headquarters in Burbank. She is a member of the Board of Directors of the Cancer Center of Santa Barbara. In addition, Alison and Geoff have generously funded the Rusack Coastal Studies Fellowships at Bowdoin College's Coastal Studies Center in Maine, and are actively pursuing a way to link marine research and conservation from the northeast to the southwest coasts of the United States through interaction between Bowdoin and the USC Wrigley Institute.

Alison Wrigley Rusack.

Alison's husband, Geoff, is the current Chairman of the Santa Catalina Island Conservancy Board of Directors and a member of the Santa Catalina Island Company Board. With his background as a lawyer, Geoff is an energetic and inquisitive voice in Board deliberations. As a consequence of Alison and Geoff's ownership of a successful vineyard and winery, they bring a practical "small business" ownership perspective to their involvement with Santa Catalina Island and the SCI Co.

Ronald Doutt, President and COO of the Santa Catalina Island Company has worked with Alison during his tenure with the Company. He said "Alison is a gracious, thoughtful woman. With homes in both Avalon and Santa Barbara, she brings a lifetime love for Catalina to the table and has a thorough grounding in the issues, opportunities and needs of Catalina that not only comes from her experiences but also from her father and grandfather. Alison, for many years, was SCICo's El Rancho Escondido manager. Just like the rest of us, at budget time she, too, went 'through the ringer' with her father to justify projects, payroll and other expenses. This seems to be a Wrigley family trait – to learn in the crucible of fire, rather than have business titles bestowed. As I understand it, Philip nurtured Bill Wrigley in this manner and Bill Wrigley, in turn, similarly taught Alison."

Alison and Geoff have exciting plans for El Rancho Escondido in the future, bringing together their love of horses, wine and the natural beauty and conservation of Catalina in the ranch's picturesque and historical location. They are also renovating Casa del Monte, originally the home of her grandparents, Philip and Helen Wrigley, to be one of the jewels of Avalon. Their greatest joy, however, is spending time on Catalina with their three sons – Hunter, Austin and Parker – who also share their family's love for the magic of Catalina.

Ada Elizabeth Wrigley and granddaughter Ada Blanche.

Grandpa A.G. Cox "Grandpa Cox" with Deedie and Blanny at a barbeque, El Rancho Escondido, Catalina.

Philip Wrigley on the lawn of El Rancho Escondido.

"Grandpa Cox" with Deedie on the left and Blanny on the right.

Dorothy Offield and Betty Offield on an island outing.

Blanny and Deedie Wrigley at Mt. Ada.

Philip and Ada Elizabeth Wrigley on Catalina.

Ada Elizabeth Wrigley on the beach at Avalon.

Ada Elizabeth Wrigley strolling the Steamer Pier.

Sock Hettler, Jim Offield, Erminie Hettler, Olive Atwater, Deedie, Ada Blanche in Little Harbor, Catalina.

Helen Atwater Wrigley at Casa del Monte in Avalon.

Philip Wrigley at El Rancho Escondido with Packard automotive.

Helen Wrigley aboard the cabin cruiser WASP at the Isthmus.

Blanny, Helen, Deedie, and Grandpa Cox at Mt. Ada in Avalon.

Helen Wrigley relaxing at Casa del Monte in Avalon.

Helen at El Rancho Escondido.

Ada Elizabeth Wrigley in the dining room at Mt. Ada.

Philip with camera, one of his many hobbies.

Helen, Deedie and Blanny celebrating Ada Blanche (Blanny) Wrigley's birthday at Casa del Monte in Avalon.

Helen Wrigley drives the family station wagon on Catalina.

Left to right, Philip K. Wrigley, Vivian and Eva Duncan, Olive Getz.

Helen Wrigley, wife of Philip K. Wrigley.

Betty Offield over looking Avalon Bay from balcony of the Wrigley home at Mt. Ada.

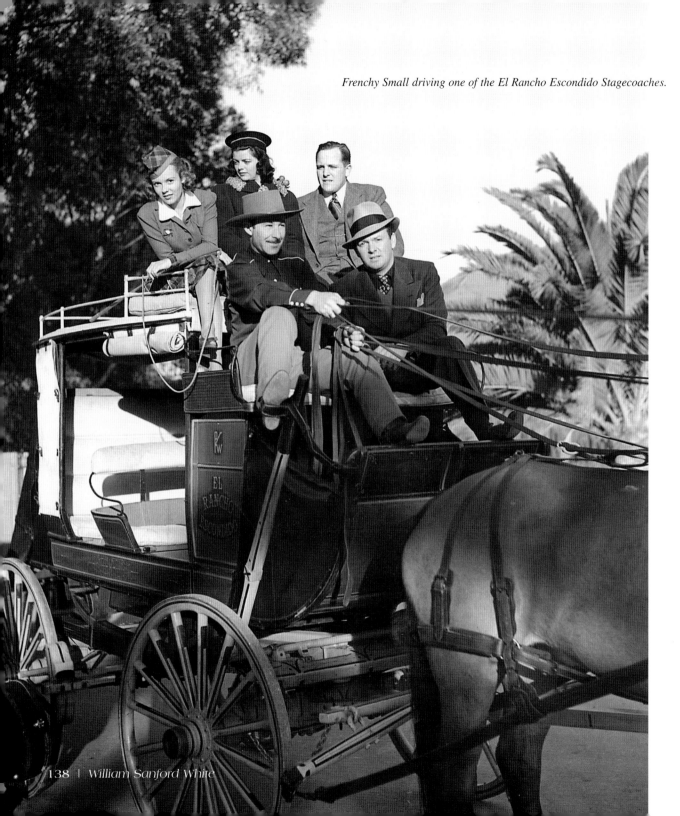

Frenchy Small driving one of the El Rancho Escondido Stagecoaches.

Dorothy Wrigley Offield.

Dorothy Wrigley, age 5.

Ada Blanche Wrigley's first car, English Standard Swallow.

Philip Wrigley and family members waiting for Avalon parade to start in front of Boos Brothers Cafeteria on Crescent Avenue.

William "Bill" Wrigley and his daughter, Alison Wrigley Rusack, in front of the fireplace at Casa del Monte in Avalon.

Philip K. Wrigley "Dad" on Khorshed.

Ada Elizabeth, Betty Offield, Dorothy Wrigley (Offield), and Bud Offield.

David M. Renton and Wrigley "Bud" Offield at Catalina Island School for Boys, 1931.

Blanny and friend.

Dorothy Wrigley age 12.

Dorothy Wrigley in 1897.

Philip K. Wrigley at 9 years old.

Top Row: Wrigley "Bud" Offield, Bill Wrigley, Philip, Emmons Sullivan.
Seated: Helen, Blanny, Deedie, Betty Offield Sullivan, Dorothy and James Offield.

Ada Elizabeth Wrigley.

Philip practicing his swing on the golf course in Avalon Canyon.

Blanny and Philip on horseback in Avalon.

James R. Offield, husband of Dorothy Wrigley Offield.

Clockwise from lower left, Helen Rosberg, Husband James, Son Will DeGray and daughter Ali DeGray.

Wrigley 'Bud' Offield, at left, with Boy Scout Troop, Catalina Island School for Boys, 1930-31.

Deedie, Wrigley "Bud," and Blanny riding in the desert outside the Wrigley family compound in Phoenix, Arizona.

Edna Jean, James, Wrigley, and Dorothy Offield, with Ada Elizabeth Wrigley seated.

Susan Hagenah, Philip K., Byron Wrigley, Phil Hagenah at Pebbly Beach Air Terminal, Catalina Island – 1969.

☙ Epilogue ☙

The Wrigleys are an American family like any other. As a family and as individuals they have experienced tremendous joy, high adventure, huge disappointment, intense grief and all the stacks in between. Through it all, love for each other, love for their country and love for this island has created an ongoing legacy. The Island is in their blood, and they are the life's blood of the Island. The three principal leaders – William Jr., Philip and Bill – have insured that the Wrigley Family Legacy will live on through the ages on their Magic Isle.

William Wrigley, Jr. and his wife, Ada Elizabeth had a vision for Santa Catalina Island in 1919 ... that it should be a "playground for all, rich or poor, youth or aged. All classes mix with democratic spirit." It was a vision of growth and community.

Care of the island was passed down to Philip Knight and Helen Atwater Wrigley. Their legacy of preservation and protection is seen in the renovations of Avalon over the decades and the creation of a sanctuary of conservation.

Bill Wrigley continued the family legacy of education and conservation, guaranteeing that future generations will be able to enjoy this beautiful island as envisioned by his grandparents. Under his guidance the Wrigley Institute for Environmental Studies has grown and thrives. Bill and his sisters, Ada Blanche and Dorothy Atwater, grew up in the shelter of the Island. Subsequent generations are now finding their place in the legacy.

The legacy is alive and growing!

☙

CREDIT & ACKNOWLEDGEMENTS

Carl & Lora Bennitt
Robbie & Christie Bos
Leon Calloway
Peggy Chan
Diane Conover
Harvey Cowell
Jean Crow
Nick Curry
Andy & Vernice Dagosta
Shirley Davy
Anthony Dolinski
Ronald & Barbara Doutt
Kelly Espinosa
Virginia French
Sidney Gally
David Gaon
Rose Ellen & David Gardner
Linda Garvey
George & Barbara Goodall
Wayne & Susie Griffin
Linda Gunderson
William Haefliger
Blanny Avalon Hagenah
Philip & Susan Hagenah
Clifford Hague
Gail Hodge
Ernie & Pat Hovard
Elena Josefe
Ellen Kelly
Fred Kilbride
George Kritzman
Chuck Liddell
Gina Long

Robert Magnuson
Mitchell Mardesich
Shirley Merriman
Dr. Tony Michaels
Patricia Ann & Bruce Moore
Dr. Ann Muscat
Paxson H. Offield
Stacey Otte
Cathie Lou Parker
Jean Paule
Jeannine Pedersen
Tim & Mickey Pitroff
Franklin Pyke
Christian Quincy
Joseph Quinn
Sam & Betty Rikalo
John Robinson
Helen & James Rosburg
Jerry Rosengren
Dr. Steven Sample
Mike Sanborn
Ada Blanche & Charles Schreiner
Steven Schreiner
Hugh "Bud" & Marie Smith
Danny & Lisa Squire
Lillian Stone
Katherine Tatis
Steven Kern Tice
Marie Whittington
Helen Wilson
Geoff & Alison Wrigley-Rusack
Misdee Wrigley

ORGANIZATIONS:
Banning Residence Museum
Catalina Island Museum Society, Inc.
The Historical Research Center,
        Boynton Beach, Florida
Huntington Advertising & Public Relations
        Patricia Rosengren, Principle
Huntington Library
Occidental College
Pasadena Museum
San Pedro Bay Historical Society
Santa Catalina Island Company
Santa Catalina Island Conservancy
Southwest Museum
The Westerners, Los Angeles Corral
Workman & Temple Family
        Homestead Museum

PHOTOGRAPHIC CREDITS TO:
Banning Residence Museum
Leon Calloway
Catalina Island Museum Society, Inc.
Antoni Dolinski
Phil Hagenah
Fred Kilbride
Paxson H. Offield
Santa Catalina Island Company
Ada Blanche & Charles Schreiner
Steven Schreiner
Hugh "Bud" Smith
Lillian Stone
Jack & Nora Tucey
Geoff Rusack and Alison Wrigley-Rusack

❧ SPECIAL THANKS ❧

Dorothy & Ben Abril
Rose & Joe Arno
Bud Avery
William P. Banning Jr.
Kurt Becker
Marge & Julian Besel
Audrey & Doug Bombard
Gertrude & Alfred Bombard
Susan Bray
Dorothy Castro
Albert Chavez
Susan & Roger Churton
John Cornell
Beth & Tod Corrin
Arthur & Marie Emerson
Krista Foster
Juanita & Howard Fraeser
Steve & Tracey Gesiriech
David & Mary Gibson
Bonnie & Loren Grey
Joseph & Jay Guion
Everett & Anna Hager
Ed & Donna Harrison
Greg & Carrie Haskin
Robert & Dorothy Hubbard
Gage & Nancy Illo
Payton & Marge Jordan
George & Kelly Juett
Richard Kellogg
George Kritzman
Jim Lauren
Elizabeth Lawton
Keith Lefever

William Leisk
Joseph & Joanne Lesser
Eunice Low
Jessie MacClanahan
Russell & Irene McClanahan
John (Marincovich) Marin
Richard & Francine Meza
Doug & Katie Miller
Jean & William Morris, Jr.
Jerry Newcomb
Norton & Peggy Norris
Morgan & Betty Odell
Robert & Virginia Odell
Ellen Pirok
Millie Poindexter
Malcolm & Carolyn Renton
Ward Ritchie
Charles & Hally Rubsamen
Lolo, Frank & Sylvester Saldana
Marcelino Saucedo
Barbara Blake Scott
Jim & Wendy Softly
Kim & Donald Stotts
Henry & Eloise Swenerton
Martha Taylor
Ailene Theime
Uncle Al Thompson
George Throop
Hugh & Katherine Tolford
James Trout Jr.
Tasha Tudor
Gladys & Walter Victor
Sherri Walker

Dwayne Walsworth
Margaret & Harold Warner
Scott & Pat Wauben
Herbert & Mildred Wegmann
Courtney Carter White
John J. & Frances White
Martha J. White
Martha H. & Tregan L. White
Roland White & Lucille Andreason
Scott & Pamela White
Taylor & Paula White
Warren & Cindy White
Wilbur & Margaret White
Robert & Betsy Williams
John & Jean Windle
Gerry Linnes Woodruff
Mary Lou & Walter Wurtman
Lewis & Betty Zeiller

❦ Bibliography ❦

Doutt, Ronald C. *Water Lines*, 3rd Quarter 2005, "Personal Remembrances – The Roles of William Wrigley and Paxson Offield...," p. 1+.

Fortune, April 1933, "William Wrigley, Jr., American," p. 84+.

Fortune, April 1933, "The Chewing Gum Industry," p. 87+.

Kowet, Don. *Chicago* (magazine), June 1977, "P.K. Wrigley: incorrigible innovator, reluctant prince," p. 138+.

Meyerhoff, Arthur E. *The Personality and Principles of Philip K. Wrigley*, limited private publication, c. 1978.

Mione, Leeann. *Saddle Horse Report*, Nov. 17, 2003. "A Big Piece of Heaven in the Bluegrass," p. 24-29.

Pacific Maritime, April 1994, "Wilmington Transportation Company," p. 18-30.

Pedersen, Jeannine. *Catalina Island (Images of America Series)* Arcadia Publishing, Charleston, SC, 2004.

Smith, Dean. *Tall Shadows: the Story of the Getz Family and Globe Corporation*, Scottsdale, AZ, 1993.

Water Lines, 1st Quarter 1994, "Santa Catalina Island Company: The First Quarter Century," p. 1+.

Water Lines, 2nd Quarter 1994, "Santa Catalina Island Company: 1919 - 1944," p. 1+.

Water Lines, 3rd Quarter 1994, "SCICo's Third Quarter Century: 1944 - 1969," p. 1+.

Water Lines, 4th Quarter 1994, "SCICo's Fourth Quarter Century: 1969 -1999," p. 1+.

Water Lines, 1994 Special Edition, "Philip Wrigley's Other Pursuits," p. 1+.

Water Lines, 1994 Special Edition, "Other Personal Remembrances of Philip K. Wrigley," p. 7+.

Waves (magazine), Fall 1999, "William Wrigley, 1933 – 1999, leaves a legacy of philanthropy," p. 1+.

Weinrott, Lester. *Chicago* (magazine), June 1977, "Sitting in at the Wrigley Round Table," p. 140+.

White, William S. and Tice, Steven K. *Santa Catalina Island: Its Magic, People, and History*, City of Industry, CA, 1997.

White, William S. *Santa Catalina Island Goes to War: World War II 1941 – 1945*, City of Industry, CA, 2001.

Windle, Ernest. *Windle's History of Santa Catalina Island*, Avalon, CA, 1949.

Wrigley-Rusack, Alison. *The Catalina Explorer* (magazine), July 1986, "El Rancho Escondido: The Early Years," p. 10+.

Wrigley-Rusack, Alison. *The Catalina Explorer* (magazine), August 1986, "El Rancho Escondido: On the Show Circuit," p. 10+.

Wrigley-Rusack, Alison. *The Catalina Explorer* (magazine), October 1986, "El Rancho Escondido: Continuing the Vision," p.7+.

☙ Index ☙

References to text are in regular **typeface.**
References to pictorial material are in *italic* **typeface.**

The **Wrigley** Family
A Legacy of Leadership in Santa Catalina Island

❧ REFERENCES TO TEXT & PICTORIAL MATERIAL ❧